E. Nathan Manning

HESIOD AND THE HEBREWS

THE GREEKS, THE HEBREWS, AND THE WESTERN VIEW OF NATURE

VDM Verlag Dr. Müller

Impressum/Imprint (nur für Deutschland/ only for Germany)
Bibliografische Information der Deutschen Nationalbibliothek: Die Deutsche Nationalbibliothek verzeichnet diese Publikation in der Deutschen Nationalbibliografie; detaillierte bibliografische Daten sind im Internet über http://dnb.d-nb.de abrufbar.

Alle in diesem Buch genannten Marken und Produktnamen unterliegen warenzeichen-, marken- oder patentrechtlichem Schutz bzw. sind Warenzeichen oder eingetragene Warenzeichen der jeweiligen Inhaber. Die Wiedergabe von Marken, Produktnamen, Gebrauchsnamen, Handelsnamen, Warenbezeichnungen u.s.w. in diesem Werk berechtigt auch ohne besondere Kennzeichnung nicht zu der Annahme, dass solche Namen im Sinne der Warenzeichen- und Markenschutzgesetzgebung als frei zu betrachten wären und daher von jedermann benutzt werden dürften.

Coverbild: www.ingimage.com

Verlag: VDM Verlag Dr. Müller Aktiengesellschaft & Co. KG
Dudweiler Landstr. 99, 66123 Saarbrücken, Deutschland
Telefon +49 681 9100-698, Telefax +49 681 9100-988
Email: info@vdm-verlag.de

Herstellung in Deutschland:
Schaltungsdienst Lange o.H.G., Berlin
Books on Demand GmbH, Norderstedt
Reha GmbH, Saarbrücken
Amazon Distribution GmbH, Leipzig
ISBN: 978-3-639-14820-6

Imprint (only for USA, GB)
Bibliographic information published by the Deutsche Nationalbibliothek: The Deutsche Nationalbibliothek lists this publication in the Deutsche Nationalbibliografie; detailed bibliographic data are available in the Internet at http://dnb.d-nb.de.

Any brand names and product names mentioned in this book are subject to trademark, brand or patent protection and are trademarks or registered trademarks of their respective holders. The use of brand names, product names, common names, trade names, product descriptions etc. even without a particular marking in this works is in no way to be construed to mean that such names may be regarded as unrestricted in respect of trademark and brand protection legislation and could thus be used by anyone.

Cover image: www.ingimage.com

Publisher: VDM Verlag Dr. Müller Aktiengesellschaft & Co. KG
Dudweiler Landstr. 99, 66123 Saarbrücken, Germany
Phone +49 681 9100-698, Fax +49 681 9100-988
Email: info@vdm-publishing.com

Printed in the U.S.A.
Printed in the U.K. by (see last page)
ISBN: 978-3-639-14820-6

Copyright © 2010 by the author and VDM Verlag Dr. Müller Aktiengesellschaft & Co. KG and licensors
All rights reserved. Saarbrücken 2010

μοῦσαι Πιερίηθεν ἀοιδῆσιν κλείουσαι
δεῦτε, Δί' ἐννέπετε, σφέτερον πατέρ' ὑμνείουσαι·

To my parents, who have always believed in me.

TABLE OF CONTENTS

INTRODUCTION

MAPS

CHAPTER 1: HESIOD
CHAPTER 2: WORKS AND DAYS
CHAPTER 3: CRITICISM ON THE POEM
CHAPTER 4: THE HEBREWS
CHAPTER 5: THE BOOK OF PROVERBS
CHAPTER 6: CRITICISM ON PROVERBS
CHAPTER 7: THE WESTERN VIEW OF NATURE
CHAPTER 8: CONCLUSION

APPENDICES
WORKS CITED
BIBLIOGRAPHIES
NOTES

INTRODUCTION

The main hypothesis that I advance in this book is that there are similarities between early Greek culture and early Hebrew culture. I think that this is solid, and if this is the only subject that it raises then I will reach my goal.

I argue in particular that this characterization applies to the views of nature of these two cultures, and use as my evidence two representative texts: Hesiod's *Works and Days* and the Book of Proverbs in the Old Testament.

Lastly, I think that the environment is an important issue. I believe that there is a modern environmental crisis—which I define more as a separation of people from nature than specific problems per se—and I attempt to resolve some aspects of it by extrapolating my texts onto the broader context of Western intellectual history.

This book is a revised version of my MA thesis, and so I would particularly like to thank Dr. Greg Stone, Director of the Interdepartmental Program in Comparative Literature and Chair of the Department of French Studies at Louisiana State University, who gave me the opportunity to study and guided my research.

Nathan Manning- Calgary, Alberta, June 2009

MAPS[†]

THE ANCIENT AEGEAN

[†] Maps courtesy of Ancient World Mapping Center, University of North Carolina at Chapel Hill (www.unc.edu/awmc)

THE ANCIENT NEAR EAST

CHAPTER 1: HESIOD

I start this study with the ancient Greek poet Hesiod, and his poem *Works and Days* (c. 700 BC). A sketch of the historical background of the Greek world prior to this period hopefully gets the ball rolling.

In the period before and during the time of Hesiod, the Greek world was emerging from what some scholars refer to as the Greek "Dark Ages", a period sandwiched between the Mycenaean Period (c.1600-1200 BC) and the Archaic Period (c.700-480 BC).

The Mycenaean period provides us with an example of a civilization that rose and fell very markedly. It achieved numerous developments—but it did not rise to a notable point of political consolidation. It was a politically fractured civilization, in which large palace-estates dominated the political and economic landscape, with peasants or serfs working the land for palace rulers. Texts written in a script that Classical scholars refer to as Linear B do not make the palace system crystal clear, but it appears that the estates had specialized economies based on the cultivation of a few crops, and a system of land-ownership that consisted of palace control either directly or through some form of lease.[1]

But around 1200-1150 BC Mycenaean civilization experienced a systems collapse. The causes of this are still debated, but one prominent Classicist characterizes the period that followed the collapse as "a slate wiped clean".[2] Others have argued for relatively more continuity, while still characterizing it as a "trough".[3] But in any case a large disturbance and disintegration of political organization and land-ownership occurred.

Following the collapse of Mycenaen civilization around 1200-1150 BC, Greece plunged into the Greek Dark Ages from c.1100-800 BC. During this time mainland Greece shows evidence of having been drastically depopulated.[4] The Dark Ages in Greece were dominated by chieftains who engaged in herding and raiding.[5]

But in the eighth century the Greeks began to settle down again—and for some reason did not do so along the lines of the large estates of the Mycenaen period. One scholar feels confident enough to paint this picture, "The end of the Greek Dark Ages was a rare time in History. A period of fluidity in, and opportunity for, land ownership, it was an era where competence and work, not mere inherited wealth and birth, might now become criteria for economic success."[6] Population growth was concomitant with more intensive agriculture, in turn stimulating greater and greater land use, and the formation of towns and cities.[7] Another scholar calls it a "...dramatic transformation. Mainland Greece suddenly goes through a period of rapid social, economic, and cultural change."[8]

This leads us into a discussion of the Archaic period, also referred to as the "polis" period, which is the period of the rise of the Greek city-states (c.700-480 BC), and the period from which the texts of Hesiod and Homer come to us.

Our sources of information for the pre-Archaic period are primarily archeological, although there is ongoing argumentation among Classicists as to whether or not the poetry of Homer describes more the culture of Mycenaen Greece, the following Dark Ages, or the later Archaic Period. In recent scholarship Homer, who traditionally was mostly thought to be the guide to either Mycenaen or Dark Age Greece, has been shown to shed light on the Archaic period.[9]

It is lamentable that a thorough analysis of Homer is simply too great a subject for me to enter into fully here. The *Iliad* and the *Odyssey* are not primarily about the natural world or people's interaction with it, and in general are preoccupied with the relatively more sensationalistic subjects of war in the former, and the journey and struggles of a hero in the latter. If anywhere in Homer does provide particular fodder for ecocritical analysis, it would be the end of the Odyssey, when Odysseus returns home to his agricultural estate in Ithaca (Bk. XIV-XXIV), particularly BK. XXIII. Book twenty-three contains the one instance in Homer that I will look at here.

This instance is Homer's use in the *Odyssey* of the olive tree metaphor (Bk. XXIII.202-230) as the cornerstone (or corner-tree) of Odysseus's house and bed. The *Odyssey* is a story of a hero's return from war, and the reestablishment of social, political, and economic order (civilization) after a time of chaos. The two-pronged role of the olive tree is significant: it formed the cornerpost of the bed, which has sexual and social connotations, and it upheld the physical structure of the house, which has economic and political connotations. We are apparently to understand from his use of the tree, that the poet was conscious of and believed in the importance of a fundamental connection between civilization and the natural world, and that in Greek culture this connection was through cultivated nature.

It is also significant—if Homer is the voice of the early Greek city-state as some have suggested—that Greek *urban* society was conscious of this fact. This metaphor suggests that though the Greek world in the Archaic period boasted an increasingly urbane culture that this culture was still very close to and conscious of the centrality of nature to civilization. And this is understandable given the close physical proximity of the countryside to the centers of even the largest Greek cities. Estimates of the rural-urban population split in Greece during the city-state period still put the population at between 65-95 % rural.[10] This is an important statistic to recall throughout the course of this study. Not until modern times has it been possible for the majority of the urban population to be beyond walking distance of fields and farms. So the presence of this knowledge in Homer is perhaps not surprising.[11]

Some may object that the olive tree metaphor is using a tree, and not fields or agriculture per se, as the cornerstone around which civilization is built. This has some weight, but I would balance it with the prominence of arboriculture and viticulture in Greek culture and farm operations. The Greeks were great cultivators of vines, and olive and fruit trees, and they enshrined their role in religious mythology and observance. In Athens, for instance, the olive tree was sacred to the city's primary goddess Athena, one of which she supposedly planted in Attica, and certain olive groves were shrines to the goddess and protected by the Athenian state. In actual practice, a small Greek farm consisted of fields as well as orchards and vineyards, all contributing in season to the family's diet and survival. Hesiod himself shows us an example of this when besides the presence of cereal agriculture he gives advice on when to harvest grapes (611).

In summary of this foray into Homer, ecocritical analysis of the Odyssey, and less so the Iliad, can contribute to a fuller understanding of the Greek view of nature by serving as a source of comparison for other more explicit and factual primary sources for the Archaic period (c.700-480 BC).

Moving on, it is indicative of Greek civilization that of the two colossi of early Greek literature—Homer and Hesiod—one, Hesiod, exhibits such a rural identity.

Hesiod relates to us in *Works and Days* that his father was something of a pioneer. He tells us (637) that his father left Asia Minor to try and escape poverty and after spending time as a sailor (634) settled on land near the town of Ascra in Boeotia, the territory of the city of Thebes on the Greek mainland (see Maps). Cheap land must have been available for settlement otherwise a man of little means like Hesiod's father could not have obtained property there. It is for this reason that the family farm probably occupied marginal land. The climate there is dry and Mediterranean, with the mountainous terrain permitting only dry-land farming (no large-scale irrigation) where farmers are dependent on seasonal rains for survival. David W. Tandy and Walter C. Neale cite an estimate of average farm size in Boeotia around that time at twenty arable acres.[12] But this estimate of overall farm size comes in high compared to other estimates of farm size in the countrysides of other Greek city-states. The Russian scholar V.N.

Andreyev reviewed inscribed public land sale records in Attica in the fifth century BC (for which we have more information) and put the standard plot size at between a mere 1.8-13.3 acres.[13] Victor Davis Hanson advances that a "normative" Attic farm covered between ten and twenty acres.[14] And M.I. Finley concluded that 45-70 acre holdings, though not unusual, were above average.[15] In almost no case until Hellenistic and Roman times do we hear of anyone's land surpassing 100 acres.[16] In terms of population, estimates for Boeotia put it at around 165,000 for the late fifth century, or a density of 70 people/km square.[17] I have already mentioned the large percentage of the rural population vis-à-vis the urban.

So life was to a great extent survival for Hesiod, and evidence from the poem shows that he has no romantic notions of farming and rural life, or poverty going together with human happiness. He calls Ascra, "a miserable hamlet" (639), a place "bad in winter, sultry in summer, and good at no time" (640).[18] As a reading of the poem shows, Hesiod portrays farming as a hard but honest and respectable occupation.

CHAPTER 2: WORKS AND DAYS

Works and Days is a short poem as compared to the Homeric epics and divides into three sections: the first section (lines 1-201) is a brief narrative of the history of the relations of humans with the gods; the second section however (202-765), which takes up the majority of the poem's 828 lines, consists of explicit practical advice on work in an agricultural context; the third section (765-828) is a random compendium of rural lore.[19]

The poem begins with an invocation of the Muses of Pieria to come hither and help the poet sing the praise of Zeus (1-4). Such an overt act of consecration (Pieria was a sacred spring on the slopes on Mount Olympus), and the subject of the first section as a whole, would seem out of place in a practical twenty-first century handbook on agriculture. But while practical advice dominates the main section of the poem, Hesiod sees no incongruence in starting the poem with an overt statement on his consciousness of the divine. This implies that Hesiod saw no separation between religion and work.

Other passages expressly confirm this. Near the outset, Hesiod claims that there are two kinds of Strife: one bad, but one good. The bad kind fosters evil war and battle (13-14), but the good kind Zeus himself has put "in the roots of the earth" (19). This "strife" is good for man for two reasons: firstly because it appeases the gods, and secondly, because it makes man work and vie with his neighbor for wealth and prosperity (21). Line 43 then reads, "For the gods keep hidden from men the means of life (42)"...or else (my paraphrase) men would become lazy and slovenly (43-44). And in a central passage Hesiod reiterates his philosophy of work by saying point blank: κὰι ἐργαζόμενοι πολὺ φίλτεροι ἀθανάτοι (308-309). Tandy and Neale translate this "the man who works is much dearer to the deathless ones (309)." Clearly these passages demonstrate a connection in the poet's mind between work and religion, and that the way a man works is an important expression of his religious beliefs. Furthermore, Hesiod also wrote the *Theogony*, the greatest compendium and synthesis of Greek mythology. That he wrote both poems adds to the impression that the two were congruent in his mind.

But is Hesiod speaking in line 309 of people in any kind of work, or specifically agriculture? The answer lies in the context of line 309 in the passage (293-320). The context is one in which the poet is enjoining his brother Perses to work, and he is clearly speaking about agriculture. Lines 299-300 contrast hunger with a barn filled with the blessings of Demeter, and the line immediately preceding line 309 refers to flocks (308). So clearly the context of lines 308-309 indicates that Hesiod is referring to those working the land.

But in the passage in which the previously noted line 41 occurs, Hesiod goes on to say, "This strife is wholesome for men. And potter is angry with potter, and craftsman with craftsman, and beggar is jealous of beggar, and minstrel of minstrel." There Hesiod is speaking about the gods' intentions with respect to hard work in general, and that this applies to all occupations—but in 308-309, Hesiod is speaking specifically about farming. So Hesiod's overall view of the scheme of things includes other kinds of work, but retains a unique status for agriculture.

Another point regarding one of these passages is important for its environmental implications. In the passage on the good kind of strife, Hesiod's expression for what one is striving for is "craving wealth" (23). At first glance this casts Hesiod in the role of the greedy industrial magnate or unscrupulous CEO. Such characterizations, however, are not the case here, because in context this phrase communicates not greediness but a genuine *need* of "wealth", and reminds us that in an agricultural economy what people call "wealth" we today would probably label "poverty", that is, something above but still primarily focused on subsistence. We should recall that Hesiod's father settled in Ascra to flee poverty (πενίη) (637, also 717), and that the poet early on ironically praises a meal of mallow and asphodel (41), the Greek equivalent of a bowl of porridge.[20] All indications are therefore that for Hesiod wealth means first survival. Eminent Classical scholar Hermann Fränkel was also of this view.[21]

Moving on in the first section, Hesiod lists the ages of men, starting with the golden age, the silver age, and thirdly the iron age. This third group was "a brazen race, sprung from ash-trees; it was in no way equal to the silver age, but was terrible and strong; they loved the lamentable works of Ares and deeds of violence; they ate no bread…" (146-147). This passage is noteworthy here for giving insight into the Greek view of non-agricultural peoples. Hesiod, for his part focuses on the connection between these people and war, and also the flip side, that those who do eat bread are apparently relatively more peaceful. Men in Hesiod are elsewhere called, "men who eat bread" (82).[22] Clearly lines 82 and 147 are in juxtaposition. This argues that Hesiod's cultural identity in relation to other people groups was related to farming.[23]

Hesiod puts the emphasis more on the relationship between agricultural people and war, but in the *Odyssey*, Homer asserts the connection between cultivated nature and civilization in a clearer light. This is in the well-known story of the Cyclops. Odysseus says of them:

> We came to the land of the Cyclops race, arrogant lawless beings who leave their livelihoods to the deathless gods and never use their own hands to sow or plough…They have no assemblies to debate in, they have no ancestral ordinances; they live in arching caves on the tops of hills, and the head of each family heeds no other, but makes his own ordinances for wife and children. (*Odyssey* IX.113-124).

Clearly this is associating a lack of agriculture with barbarism. Robin Osborne agrees that the Cyclops in Homer is "the inversion of the Greek life of farming and political activity."[24] The mention of the Cyclopes not working with their own hands also stands out.[25] This is a subject that I will look at now in detail in Hesiod and later on in the book of Proverbs.

A pivotal question here is whether or not Hesiod actually did physical work himself and considered it to be honorable. In a recent study, Stephanie A. Nelson asserts (in the second respect) that he did not, stating: "The Greeks were remarkably free from the idea that the sweat of one's brow is ennobling. Hesiod himself, despite the more romantic view of some commentators, sees work as simply a necessary evil."[26] I disagree with this interpretation and will adduce several passages from the text of *Works and Days* to advance my argument.

To begin with, Hesiod's belief that the gods have a say in the occupations of man must apply here. If the gods intended man to work primarily in agriculture then it must be no disgrace for him to actually do the work. Besides the passage on Strife (11-26) that has already been discussed, the first reference in the text that confirms this is Hesiod's use of the word ἀρετή in a passage (286-294) in which he is speaking about work and the gods. Liddell and Scott translate ἀρετή in an active sense as, "goodness, excellence, especially of manly qualities, manhood, valor, prowess", and in a moral sense as, "goodness, virtue, merit etc…" This is obviously a word with noble connotations. And Hesiod uses it in the context of an explicit reference to "sweat" on line 289. Hesiod says, "Badness can be got easily and in shoals: the road to her is smooth, and she lives very near us. But between us and Goodness (ἀρετή) the gods have placed the sweat of our brows (ἰδρῶτα)….(287-290)" Tandy and Neale translate this passage, "It is easy to seize failure, and in quantities; the road is smooth: she resides very near. But before success (ἀρετή) the deathless gods put sweat: long and straight up is the path to her and tough at first (287-291)." I contend that Hesiod's use ἰδρῶτα in this passage communicates that he includes physical work in his view of ἀρετή.

13

Although she does not mention this explicitly, I think it is safe to say that Nelson would probably take Hesiod's use of "sweat" here to be metaphorical. In reference to this, while the word here is almost certainly also intended to be a metaphor for hard work broadly defined, to assert that ἱδρῶτα is wholly metaphorical, that Hesiod intends absolutely no evocation of physical work, is almost certainly taking a secondary interpretation. The first reason for this is his choice of the word. He could have used ἔργον, or any other word to represent "work." But he chose "sweat". Secondly the context of the passage within the poem confirms a literal reading. In line 304, Hesiod goes on to pontificate on indigents, in his words "the stingless drones who wear away the labor of the bees by eating, idlers that they are (304)." If he intends to sit around himself, it is incongruous and hypocritical for Hesiod forthrightly to condemn indigents!

Nevertheless, the metaphorical interpretation demands further explanation and in turn throws the discussion onto clarifying the practice of Hesiod's belief, in other words onto determining whether the man that the Archaic Greeks held as exemplary not only believed "work" to be ennobling but actually worked physically himself—or whether he simply administered and supervised the work of others, either servants or slaves.

Considering the evidence, although Hesiod undoubtedly exemplifies elements of a "supervisory role", the text shows that he does also exemplify that he worked himself physically, and practiced what he preached. That he evidences the first is proven by his many references to planning and directing the work of slaves (406, 459, 470, 502, 597, 766).[27] Now the purpose of my analysis here is not to enter into an apology of slavery—but in one of these passages (458-461), Hesiod portrays the farmer working alongside, *in the same way as*, his slaves.[28] Evelyn-White translates this, "So soon as the time for ploughing is proclaimed to men, then make haste, you and your slaves alike, in wet and in dry, to plough in the season for ploughing, and bestir yourself early in the morning so that your fields may be full." West renders it, "As soon as the ploughing-time reveals itself to mortals, then go at it, yourself and your labourers…".[29] The line that tells us one way or the other is δὴ τότ' ἐφορμηθῆναι ὁμῶσ δμῶέσ τε καὶ αὐτὸσ (459). The verb is ἐφορμηθῆναι ("to rush at it", or "to go at it with vigour"), ὁμῶσ is an adverb "equally, likewise, alike", δμῶέσ τε καὶ αὐτὸσ, "the slaves and you." Hesiod's use of the adverb here leaves no doubt that the Greek small-farmer worked physically in the same way as his slaves.

So I maintain here—insofar as Hesiod is representative—that the text of *Works and Days* is clear on both the theory and practice of work in the Archaic Greek context.

And yet an overview of Classical scholarship from diverse periods shows that there has been a lack of discussion and conclusion on these questions among scholars, as to whether or not the man that the Archaic Greeks held as exemplary considered physical work to be ennobling and actually practiced it. This is a large subject that I will enter into more in Chapter 7 and I will just raise a few main elements of it here.

One of the main reasons for this lack of discourse in modern scholarship may be because the people who read, interpret, and teach Hesiod are scholars and intellectuals who as a group do not hold physical work to be something exemplary. This has most likely been the case since the Renaissance and the decline of Western monasticism.

Another reason for this in certain historical periods is probably what was going on in the broader society. In an age of discovery and conquest people get wealth through other means other than working the land as Hesiod proscribes. Also the valuing of physical work is rarely favourable to the ruling and patronizing class, as is the case in industrialism, and feudalism and aristocratic agrarianism. For example, the plantation owners of the antebellum South were fonder of the managerial Cato the Elder,[30] although the Southern yeoman class,[31] if they could have procured a copy of him, would probably have identified more with the industrious Hesiod and his version of agrarianism.*

In respect to this pivotal question of physical labor, if there has been a unceremonious shuffling of the discussion to dusty corners, or a discrediting of the one side through reference to the supervisory role in other Classical literature (Xenophon, Cato the Elder etc…) then Hesiod has been done a great disservice and Western civilization denied a socially acceptable archetype central to its cultural origins. In a civilized society, the establishment of a socially acceptable archetype, or hero, requires, arguably, the genius of a writer or poet, but almost certainly, and particularly for the upper classes, the validation of those entrusted with and knowledgeable of the written lore of a culture. All scholars as a group have to do is cast something as boorish, and the upper classes will not touch it with a ten-foot

---

* Please see Appendix A for an etymology of the word "agrarian" in English. See Appendix B for an explanation of the distinction between aristocratic agrarianism and middle-class agrarianism. See Appendix C for a summary of agrarian terms in Greek history.

pole. And such is the case for the most part in this instance. Thomas Hardy went a long way in finally giving rural culture in England its due, but the implications of one of his central contentions—that it was a major part of English culture and merited respect as such—did not improve the social standing of farmers in modern societies.[32] In respect to this subject it is long overdue that scholars note that the yeoman theory of work is an alternative to the industrial theory and that Hesiod and the yeoman hold real potential as a multifarious Western archetype.

Moving on once again in the text, Hesiod exhibits the trait of being very cautious to the point of shrewd skepticism about others, especially urban elites wielding political or economic power. He addresses an entire passage to local rulers (201-285). In it Hesiod inserts an example of the fable genre, an early example of it in Greek literature. Aesop's fables mostly deal with character traits, but Hesiod's is more concerned with political and economic justice. We get the sense throughout this passage that Hesiod actually has disdain for his social superiors. Although they wield more economic and political power than him, he is not intimidated by them, and in fact holds them in contempt. He thinks for himself and shows that he has pride and self-confidence. These traits—a distrust of the concentration of power and a critical mind—are essential to the functioning of a democratic state. This passage demonstrates some of the traits of the Archaic Greeks that resulted in the invention of democracy.[33]

Hesiod also shows a cardinal Greek characteristic of revering order in all things. We find this in lines 471-472, "to guard good measure is good, and even the best of all things", and in his contrast of righteousness (δίκη) with hubris (ὕβρισ) (313-314); along these lines Tandy and Neal suggest a definition of ὕβρισ as "a disregard for process".[34]

To knock off several other points that should not be missed— Hesiod shows a common sense attitude toward investment by arguing essentially, "Don't put all of your eggs in one basket," or in his words "Do not put all your goods in hollow ships" (691). He also sets the precedent for Xenophon's more enlightened discussion on the subject of marriage in the *Oeconomicus* by stating that a man can find nothing better than a good wife and nothing worse than a bad one (702-704).

But unfortunately Hesiod's misogyny definitely outweighs his other side overall. (Hesiod is, after all, our source for the story of the gods creating woman as a bane for man's involvement in Prometheus's theft of fire). In reference to this subject, this study limits itself to looking at Hesiod's relationship to the natural world and its implications, and so issues related to gender for the most part fall outside its cadre.[35] But the essential role of women in agrarianism forms an exclusive subject of study, and is necessary to determine if it is an acceptable body of thought for use in environmentalism.

In conclusion, in this chapter I have looked at examples from the text of that are important for understanding how Hesiod viewed the role of humanity in nature.

Please see the attached note for a short review of the general merits of the translations.[36]

CHAPTER 3: CRITICISM ON THE POEM

Modern scholarship on Hesiod got underway late as compared to interest in Homer, who has seen many translations and commentaries since the Renaissance. *Works and Days* in particular did not see concerted scholarly interest until the twentieth-century.[37]

Most of the scholarship on *Works and Days* in the first half of the twentieth century was German. The Classicist Ulrich von Wilamowitz-Moellendorff published his edition and commentary in 1928.[38] Tandy and Neale characterize Wilamowitz's treatment of Hesiod as "condescending,"[39] and relate that the nature of early German scholarship was predominantly philological. Werner Jaeger's *Paideia: The Ideals of Greek Culture*, a non-philological work, was first published in German in 1933. The middle of the century saw Solmsen's *Hesiod and Aeschylus* (1949), and the third chapter of Hermann Fränkel's *Early Greek Poetry and Philosophy* (1951).[40]

Jaeger's three volume work is a *chef d'oeuvre* of scholarship on Greek literature and culture, and includes a chapter on Hesiod. In his characterization of the period from which the poem originated Jaeger is nuanced. He grants that early Greece was predominantly rural,[41] but overall is strong on the parallel nature of Greek culture throughout its history. In his view, it split in the Archaic period along the lines of aristocratic and "peasant" culture, with both existing side by side. He sees Homer as communicating the ideals of the former and Hesiod those of the latter.[42] This developed further during the Classical Period with the rise of urban centers.

Jaeger knew that Greek culture stood out for being very contentious. This dynamic was in full swing in fifth century Athens in particular, which was the apex of a very high level of philosophical and cultural debate, the polemics of which are encapsulated for us in the comedies of Aristophanes and the dialogues of Plato. One of the issues to which Aristophanes applied his poetic wit was not the relations between the yeomanry and the aristocracy (the earlier bifurcation), but rather those between traditional Greece and the rising star of Socratic philosophy. Although detailed treatment of them is impossible in this study, the plays of Aristophanes (especially *Clouds*) and the works of Plato are important to an understanding of the Western view of nature because they show the social dynamics involved during this critical period.

Jaeger assumes that Hesiod lived slightly before the polis period. This places *Works and Days* slightly earlier than the more major consensus, which dates it to sometime in the eighth century BC.[43] Jaeger concludes that a pan-Hellenic Greek identity and culture did not emerge until this period, and that when it did Hesiod and the rural strand eventually lost out.[44] This would seem to be proven correct by the dominance of urban Greek culture during the Hellenistic period i.e. it was not Hesiodic culture that Alexander spread across the East but more the artistic and intellectual culture of the polis. But Jaeger reserves respect for both Hesiod and Aristophanes, the two most potent representatives of rural Greece. Apparently unlike Wilamowitz, he treats Hesiod seriously and respectfully, as an equal to Homer. The reason he did this is probably because of his assertion that Hesiod, as did Homer, stood for what had been a genuine and respectable segment of ancient Greek society. Jaeger's treatment, however, remains very broad and does not touch on economic or environmental elements.

In the instance of Solmsen's *Hesiod and Aeschylus,* of which as Jaeger's there is also an English translation, the discussion is more along the lines of literary criticism, with the majority of it focusing on *Theogony*. This study therefore highlights Hesiod the poet and not Hesiod the voice of rural Greece or Hesiod the farmer. When it does treat *Works and Days*, it is to look at Hesiod's theology and philosophy of man. There is also no place given for how the views of the poet might either have had or have economic or environmental implications.

Hermann Fränkel's work gives us more in this respect. Fränkel's work is more like Jaeger's, and consists of a broad, relatively readable study of Greek literature from Homer to Pindar. Fränkel is concerned with attempting to get at the "underlying ideas" of a work or literary period,[45] in his words, "To ascertain in its essential features the frame of mind peculiar to the epoch, and to follow up the changes it underwent in the course of time…"[46]

So Fränkel proposes to give us the essence of Hesiod, and in so doing gives more on which the twenty first century ecocritical analyst can chew. He brings out several important points, the first having to do with the poet's philosophy of work. In his words, "Hesiod is convinced that the order of labor also, like the order of nature, is established by the gods."[47] Fränkel here adduces a line in Hesiod central to this study, line 398, which says, "Foolish Perses! *Work the work which the gods ordained for men* (398), lest in bitter anguish of spirit you with your wife and children seek your livelihood amongst your neighbours, and they do not heed you (397-400)."[48] So Fränkel had already postulated the conclusion of the previous chapter of this study, that Hesiod's religious consciousness applies to how he views work. He goes on to note that Hesiod councils praying to consecrate a task only once, that being the harvest (465)—although adding that "in the Greek fashion it is natural and matter-of-fact."[49] Secondly, Fränkel points out Hesiod's close relationship with nature, citing his use of the stars and the migratory periods of birds to tell time (448, 486), as opposed to using the names of months.[50]

So Hesiod is definitely a type of Western man relatively close to nature—but Fränkel does not induce that Hesiod is a type of Western man less harmful to nature, or one more inclined to an ecological relationship with the environment. This, however, is understandable as environmental issues were not prominent when he wrote his work.

Fränkel culminated generations of German dominance in the study of Hesiod. But in the second half of the twentieth-century English-language scholarship began to pay more attention to him. This is not to say that agrarianism as an idea, or yeomanry as a class in the English speaking world had ever ceased to exist, or enjoy the championing of various political or literary figures i.e. Thomas Jefferson, William Cobbett, G.K. Chesteron etc… For a general history of such figures and their views on agrarianism see a study that is essential reading for the subject primarily because it is the only one of its kind, that being James A. Montmarquet's *The Idea of Agrarianism*.[51] Rather, this post-War trend demonstrates that agrarianism is finally beginning to receive more consideration among scholars, a phenomenon, as was touched upon earlier, that has been more the exception than the rule. The Germans appear to have initiated this and English-language scholars have increased the trend. French scholarship, which shows an emphasis on material culture, must also not be overlooked.[52] Numerous post-War English translations of Hesiod demonstrate this increased interest.[53] The championing of agrarianism by various major figures, however, does not completely explain the comparative lack of interest in Hesiod as compared to Homer until the second half of the twentieth century.

It seems also that because all civilized societies were agricultural until the Industrial Revolution, that figures of all stripes—academic, literary, and otherwise—often took it for granted. Jeremy Cohen, in his book on the history of Genesis 1:28, also stresses that pre-modern Jewish and Christian scholars did not debate the concept of human dominion in the natural world as they did other concepts in Genesis.[54]

Wendell Berry posits that until the Romantic poets of the nineteenth century, when the effects of Industrialism began to manifest themselves, that most scholars and poets alike had taken for granted that man was part of nature.[55] He therefore participated in a relatively innocent relationship with nature and did not much think of looking *at* it.[56] This is a significant assertion that I will consider more in Chapter 7.

Here, to avoid a tedious compendium of the numerous studies, I will take a thematic approach to summarizing post-War English language scholarship on Hesiod.[57]

In post-War English language scholarship in general, there has been more attention given to Hesiod's actual living environment (social, political, environmental)—as opposed to the poem as literature or philological sample. This is a helpful trend that gives background and substance to what distinguishes small freeholding farmers.

On the one hand, a previous consensus founded on a 1957 article by Édourd Will, had been that Hesiod represented the voice of small independent farmers in Boeotia homologous to those in nearby Attica.[58] We have more information about the existence and nature of this group in Attica from the surviving legislation of Solon and the larger literary corpus that formed in Athens and has survived. More recently, Victor Davis Hanson has reasserted with Wills that Hesiod bears similarities to the Attica of the time of Solon. He emphasizes that the revised Athenian constitution and laws for which Solon was known, the "patrios politeia", was recalled in later Athenian history as the great political achievement of the yeomanry, which some contrasted with later Athenian "radical democracy" that had done away with tying citizenship to land ownership.[59]

On the other hand, other recent scholarship has departed from Will, jettisoned Solon, and argued that Hesiod lived more or less independent of the city-state. This is primarily the view of Paul Millett, whom others have followed.[60] For example, Anthony T. Edwards in *Hesiod's Ascra* (2004) is of the opinion that the poem speaks more about the dynamics between the countryside and Hesiod's village (Ascra) than the countryside and the Boeotian city-state,[61] and that *Works and Days* looks back to the Dark Age and its modes of social organization more than it looks ahead to the Archaic period and the modes of the emerging polis system.[62] This would put him at odds with Fränkel and Hanson and align him more with the judgment of Jaeger on this point. He argues that the poem does not cohere with the social institutions so far offered to explain it.[63]

So the view of Will and Hanson in regard to Hesiod would see his situation as bearing similarities to the economic, political, and social system of a city-state paradigm, such as Athens, about which we know quite a bit from other sources. The Greek city-states obviously differed from city to city—politically some being more democratic and some more oligarchic or tyrannical—but this view would emphasize commonalities such as the concepts of citizenship, constitutional government, citizen armies, the rule of law, and the presence of yeomen between Boeotia and Attica. Hanson for his part goes further, seeing social similarities between Boeotia and other Greeks city-states besides Athens, such as Megara during the time of the aristocratic poet Theognis (c.550 BC).[64] So Hanson argues that Hesiod is an example of a broader, Pan-Hellenic phenomenon. But we again must keep in mind that even Hanson does not argue that Hesiod represents all of Greece, but rather that he represents one camp that existed throughout Greece.[65]

Hanson is a Classicist at California State University, Fresno, who has ruffled feathers in the Classics community for his work on early Greece. As a broad characterization he does not attempt to make his work objective historical writing, but argues his points strongly, at times vituperatively, subscribing more to the philosophy that the Classics should be made more accessible to the general population. He argues that Classicists and educators in general must teach youth the fundamentals of Western culture, and that the lessons and values of Greek and Roman history still inform current issues. He also, however, tends to overlook the deficiencies of Greek civilization (i.e. slavery, the marginalizing of women), and has a habit of needlessly discrediting his valid assertions. For example, he has compared his Classical colleagues to the Linear B scribes of the Mycenaean period, and come out strongly in favor of the war in Iraq.[66]

But regardless, Hanson has a firm grasp of the sources, and more than any other recent scholar has consistently drawn attention to the role of the "yeoman" in the development of early Greece. He states: "…the historical background of Greece, especially its democratic background, is best understood as the result of widespread agrarianism among the rural folk who were the dynamos from which the juice of Hellenic civilization flowed."[67] And there are many such statements in his work. Underlying this specific exaltation is a deep respect if not idealization of the Archaic Greeks in general (who he calls "polis Greeks") as having been as close as the civilized world has ever got to the ideal of political and economic freedom. In conclusion, Hanson's excesses are inexcusable, but in relation to this study, his work remains important and provides a litany of references to the primary sources.

A specific point of contention in post-War scholarship is what label to give Hesiod. On the one end of the scale, Alfonso Mele (1979) sees Hesiod as an aristocrat,[68] although this is certainly a peripheral view. Chester Starr (1977, 125-127) calls him a "semi-aristocrat".[69] Getting progressively more towards the middle, Ian Morris expresses probably the most dominant view in Hesiod scholarship and calls Hesiod, "the middling man incarnate...*Works and Days* is the oldest example of a peculiarly central Greek conception of the good society as a community of middling farmers."[70] Morris is a prominent twenty-first century scholar, and that he too sees the middling farmer as a peculiarly Greek conception lends further credence to my assertions in this study (although here I draw a parallel to the early Hebrew conception). Edwards, while not agreeing totally with such a view, concedes: "*Works and* Days, in fact, provides perhaps the clearest articulation in ancient Greek literature of what I elsewhere term the voice of the *agros*, the expression of the values and experiences of the rural population."[71] Hanson uses the English term "yeoman" interchangeably with the Greek term "georgos" (see also Appendix C).[72] Tandy and Neal for their part represent the usage within the social sciences of the term "peasantry";[73] they cite Robert Redfield (1953, p.31) and Paul Millett (1984, p.107) as having preceded them in the choice of this label. Thus we have "semi-aristocrat", "middling man", "yeoman", "georgos", and "peasant"— all used in post-War English language scholarship.

Although Tandy and Neal's term is accepted within the social sciences, their choice of the term "peasant" is still hard to swallow. The term "peasant" has connections to the Middle Ages and Feudalism, which differ from the Archaic Greek social, economic, and political structure in significant ways. Although peasants were the ones working the land in the Middle Ages, they rarely owned land themselves.[74] Hesiod on the other hand owned his own plot. Secondly, class distinction in the Feudal system was a pyramid with God at the top, the king, the Feudal lords, and all the way down to the peasant. The class structure in Attica (on which we are forced to rely because of the information we have on it) differed from the Medieval in that the class distinctions were tied to wealth, and not a divinely instituted hierarchy.[75] Attica from the time of the Cleisthenian reforms was divided into four classes,[76] and these distinctions were based on the amount of agricultural produce the individual citizen in question could produce off of his privately owned land (except the θῆτεσ who did not own land).[77] The Attic classification allows exact placement in one class or the other, and shows how closely associated the Attic legal and political system originally was to owning and farming land.

So in academic discourse, if a scholar is going to apply an English title to Hesiod, I advance "yeoman" in preference to "peasant" because the former in English carries the attribute of a farmer who owns his own land; although in academic writing one might as well go straight to γεωργόσ.[78]

In non-academic forums, the best term is probably "small-farmer", or possibly "yeoman" in certain situations.

It is a sign of the times, however, that the *American Heritage Dictionary* (2001) defines "yeoman" as "a member of a *former* class of small freeholding farmers in England." This shows that if scholars, filmmakers, writers, journalists etc… do not revive this word or popularize another then the idea will die out in the cultural contexts of English-speaking countries.

In summation, scholarship on Hesiod, while not as voluminous as scholarship on Homer, is still a formidable body of material to cover. Here I have tried to pick out some of it that applies.

CHAPTER 4: THE HEBREWS

As I mentioned in the Introduction, I argue that there are similarities between early Greek culture and early Hebrew culture, and that this applies to their views of nature. The Old Testament book of Proverbs stands out as being as broad a record of the Hebrew view as is found among the books of the Old Testament, and that is why I have selected it here.

To begin with, an overview of the geography and history of ancient Israel will provide the context of Hebrew view of nature and the book of Proverbs in particular.

The geography of the Levant is dry Mediterranean uplands, hills and a few peaks of higher mountains in Lebanon. The word "Levant" comes from the French *lever*, "to raise up", or *levé*, "raised up". Ancient Israel itself was mostly the hill regions, an interspersion of grassland and forested areas at higher elevations (see Maps). Such hills hold a wide range of climates and plant species in an accordion-like fashion. This encourages diversity in the domestication of plants and "transhumance" in the domestication of animals, the practice of moving livestock to different summer and winter pasture.[79] One scholar calls the original native plant mix in this geography a "smorgasbord".[80] Taken together the conditions in Canaan make it a good setting for the domestication of plants and animals and small-scale subsistence farming.[81]

Although scholarship is not conclusive in regard to dates the early centuries of Hebrew history break down as follows: the Tribal Period (c.1300-1200 BC), which is the period of the conquest and settling of Canaan;[82] the Period of the Judges (c.1200-1030 BC); and the United Kingdom of Israel (c.1020-930 BC), which begins with King Saul, extends through the rule of King David, and ends after the reign of King Solomon.[83]

The first archaeological evidence of the people of Israel in the Levant is found on the Egyptian "Merneptah Stele", which is a record of a military campaign in the region by Pharoah Merneptah (1224–1204 BC).[84] One scholar says that around 1100 BC the Israelites were still playing the role of "pioneers" in the hills of Judea and Samaria.[85] The presence of this pioneering stage forms one similarity to the period in Greek history that which preceded Hesiod.

Evan Eisenberg has done important work on the early Hebrew view of nature, which includes his essay, "The Ecology of Eden", in the Harvard collection *Judaism and Ecology*.[86] This essay contains information from his full-length book on the subject.[87]

Eisenberg sets out the Hebrew and Near Eastern conception of the Garden of Eden. He remarks that Eden from Ezekiel to Milton was considered an elevated region.[88] He notes that Genesis refers to it as the *source* of four rivers (Gen. 2.10). He then lays out the view of the early Hebrews regarding wilderness, noting that the Hebrew *gan* translates as "vegetable garden" or "fruit orchard", and that a cognate is *gan'elohim* "the garden of God", which was the Hebrew word to refer to the wooded mountains.[89]

So this view saw places of wilderness as God's garden, which indicates that the Hebrews had a conception of realms: of a realm primarily for God, and one primarily for humans. That this was connected to agriculture comes out in the term "garden." This moves one to the conclusion that the Hebrews saw God's realm as being the wilderness, where cultivation was not possible, and humanity's realm as being in those places where it was. This constitutes a fundamental aspect of the early Hebrew view of nature.

Eisenberg also brings to light the role and influence of the Canaanites in Israel's history and relation to the environment. Eisenberg holds that the Canaanites were the first farmers of the Mediterranean basin, and developed many of the agricultural methods that farmers there still use today.[90] He states that wheat and barley were originally domesticated in the Near Eastern highlands and only later transplanted to Mesopotamia.[91] He goes on to say that the Israelites were in fact resettling a Canaan that had experienced depopulation during four centuries of previous Egyptian "rule".[92]

Taking his assertions in hand, this study agrees with Eisenberg in that the Canaanites were not a negligible influence on the nation of Israel. That the Israelites were apparently able to conquer pre-established towns and cities indicates that the Canaanites were in at least military decline. But asced the book of Joshua relates in substantial detail, the Israelites took over the infrastructure of the Canaanite towns and cities.[93] So it is logical to suggest that they adopted certain of the Canaanite agricultural practices. Also, the influence of Canaanite religion on the Hebrews is one of the recurrent themes of the Old Testament.

Most scholars agree that the compilation of the book of Proverbs at least began during the reign of Solomon (c.965-931 BC), as the book states (Prov. 1.1). But the book's values and ethic did not pop up all of a sudden. They came primarily from the preceding period, the Period of the Judges, which stands out as the period of Hebrew agrarianism in its purist form. This was the nation of Israel's formative period that led up to the apex of its political consolidation and power in the region during the reigns of David and Solomon. The information on it comes to us primarily in the books of Joshua, Judges, and Ruth, sections of the historical books (I & II Samuel, I & II Kings, and I & II Chronicles) and from archaeology.

During the Judges period, the nation of Israel functioned for approximately two hundred years without centralized religious or political authority. It was a decentralized agrarian society. This system appears to have been the result of the implementation of prescriptions laid out in the Torah. Looking at it, it is clear that the Hebrew Law lays out not only a religious and political system, but also a prescription for an economic system.

A major chapter for this information is Leviticus 25. According to the economic prescriptions that this chapter lays out, every Israelite family was to own agricultural property (25.13). The land was to be divided up among the individual families of the twelve tribes, and although it could be sold, it had to revert to the ancestral owner every fifty years, during the Jubilee year (25.14). So no one could sell land permanently, let alone speculate on it, meaning that this practice of property ownership amounts essentially to one of long-term rent (fifty years). The central ideas are repeated throughout the chapter as if to leave no doubt about what is being prescribed: "When the years are many, you are to increase the price, and when the years are few, you are to decrease the price, because what he is really selling you is the number of crops" (25.16). Even property within a city is subject to a variation of this extremely rooted theory of owning property (25.29-31). This chapter also lays out contingencies relating to an Israelite who falls into poverty, lending money, and slavery (25.35-54).

But one of the most important verses in the chapter and arguably the whole Bible with regards to property-ownership and human economic activity—and therefore the relationship of man to the natural world—is the following:

> The land must not be sold permanently, because the land is mine and you are but aliens and my tenants. Throughout the country that you hold as a possession, you must provide for the redemption of the land. (Leviticus 25.23-24) [94]

The implications of these verses for Jews and Christians are staggering. They are also significant to analysis of the Judaic and Christian views of nature (see Chapter 7).

The second sentence in the passage refers to the concept of "redemption". This concept sounds strange to modern ears, and I don't want to get into it here because it is a complicated subject. Please see note for a list of its uses in the Bible.[95]

The system of the division of the land indicates that the unit of ownership that held title was the "household" and not the individual. In the Jubilee year, each individual Hebrew was to return physically to the "family property" (25.10). There is a word that designates "household",[96] which consisted of a group of around ten to thirty people led by a patriarch living in a cluster of stone or mud-brick dwellings, and a word that refers to a more extended family, or clan, that might take the form of a village.[97]

Eisenberg says, "In contrast to the plantations that sprawled across the great river valleys of the Near East, the hills nurtured a world of small holdings, painstakingly husbanded."[98] He goes on:

> The more we know about the Israelites, the clearer it is that they were Canaanite hill farmers who practiced a sophisticated and fairly sustainable mixed husbandry of grains, vines, livestock, and trees yielding fruit, nuts, and oil. They were neither desert nomads mistrustful of nature, nor proud hydraulic despots lording it over nature. They were good farmers living frugally on the margins and using the best stewardship they knew…They were not so different from present-day farmers of the Andes or of Szechwan…[99]

This comparison to South America and China might only be justified if Eisenberg were to make more of the comparison that forms the central contention of this study—that there were similarities between the ancient Israelites and the other farmers in the Mediterranean climatic zone, specifically the Archaic Greeks; although he does allude to this, stating: "They were not so different, perhaps, from other peasants of the Mediterranean basin, past and present." [100]

Eisenberg in his essay takes property ownership one step further, and makes it the defining characteristic of two types of worldviews and two types of civilizations: those composed of small-scale, relatively self-sufficient units practicing mixed husbandry, and those of large-scale, irrigated operations and large government bureaucracies.[101]

As the length of the discussion here shows, I agree with this. The system of property ownership that a society institutes has widespread social ramifications, and is a fundamental and determining element of political and economic organization. And it has significant environmental implications as well because it sets out the way a society divides up and uses its land.

When it comes to their system of property ownership and economic organization it is important to note that the Hebrews in other respects—i.e. religion, historical consciousness—saw themselves as different. When one looks at the Middle East today, apparently not much has changed. Specifically they consistently maintained that their latter, independent situation was different from their former Egyptian one. Thus it would not be out of character for the Israelites to have been conscious of the other elements of this, and to have strongly associated their own decentralized political and economic system of small-scale, independent agriculture with their overall identity.

The Old Testament elsewhere gives us evidence to confirm this. For example, after several hundred years of this decentralized society, when the Hebrew people first came to the prophet Samuel, the last of the Judges, for an alteration of the original structure, and asked him for a king, it was apparently a very grave matter:

> …this displeased Samuel; so he prayed to the Lord. And the Lord told him: 'Listen to all that the people are saying to you; it is not you they have rejected, but they have rejected me as their king. As they have done from the day I brought them up out of Egypt until this day, forsaking me and serving other gods, so they are now doing to you. Now listen to them; but warn them solemnly and let them know what the king who will reign over them will do. (I Samuel 8.9).

So God actually calls Himself the "king" of this libertarian society. I say that the "gods" here are symbolic for the political structure of the surrounding nations, or political centralization in general. God's answer is: let them have it and see where it gets them. Freedom—that is, the social and economic autonomy possible within the household-based structure of their agrarian society—will be seriously diminished. Thus in his response Samuel projects a weakening of their agrarian, free society:

> This is what the king who will reign over you will do: He will take your sons and make them serve with this chariots and horses, and they will run in front of his chariots. Some he will assign to be commanders of thousands and commanders of fifties, and others to plough his ground and reap his harvest, and still others to make weapons of war and equipment for his chariots. He will take your daughters to be perfumers and cooks and bakers. He will take the best of your fields and vineyards and olive groves and give to his attendants. He will take a tenth of your grain and of your vintage and give it to his officials and attendants. Your menservants and maidservants and the best of your cattle and donkeys he will take for his own use. He will take a tenth of your flocks, and you yourselves will become his slaves. When that day comes, you will cry out for relief from the king you have chosen, and the Lord will not answer you in that day. (I Samuel 8.11-18).

Several points deserve noting in this passage. First of all, it shows that the Hebrew prophets, and therefore Hebrew religion, were concerned with secular affairs. Samuel here is concerned about freedom in the political and economic spheres. He also shows a sensitivity to issues of slavery. Other passages from both the major and minor prophets also demonstrate that they were also conscious of the state of Israel's land.[102]

Secondly, we should note the close association of economic and political elements in this society. In an agricultural economy, if you have land ownership split up to a great extent and do not allow accumulation of property it discourages the concentration of economic power; in an industrial economy, the same applies for property (including capital) of any type. And with the ownership of property and businesses decentralized in as many hands as possible, it is more likely that individuals will be relatively more self-sufficient and in less need of outside entities. But when economic power becomes concentrated in either large estates or corporations, the self-sufficiency of individuals is diminished, tying them to someone or something that will look after them when times get tough, usually the state.[103]

This passage therefore confirms that the Hebrews originally believed that economic decentralization mitigates despotism and totalitarianism.

This leads us into the historical period during which the compilation of the book of Proverbs began, which is generally agreed upon to have been around the time of Solomon (c.970-930 BC).[104]

By the time of Solomon, only a generation removed from Samuel, three classes of teachers had developed in Hebrew society: the priests, the prophets, and the counsel of the elders (Ezekiel 7.26).[105] The priest were to adhere and make the people adhere to the Law, which regulated many social, religious, and economic aspects of Hebrew society; the prophets spoke (unlike either of the two other groups) with the phrase "thus saith the Lord"; and the council of the elders or wise imparted council on secular affairs.[106] Whatever educated influence was exercised over the compilation and re-working of Proverbs that we have bears the mark of this last group. The validity of the elders' wisdom, however, derived from harmonization with the Torah and the word of the prophets.[107] These elders filled the important role of translating the Law and the prophets into more everyday situations— and vice versa of translating down to earth wisdom into a more literary form. For this reason they were an essential link to youth,[108] and the book of Proverbs evidences a thematic emphasis on instructing especially young men on how to pass through the trials of young adulthood and learn to live a wise and prudent life.

The nation of Israel split soon after the reign of Solomon into northern and southern segments, Israel and Judah, the northern part being dispersed by the Assyrians around 730 BC, and the southern not until around 586 BC by the Babylonians. The literature that has come to us from the latter dispersal points to a melancholic longing for Jerusalem, and shows that by that time the Jews held a special affection for that city; clearly, their religion was very much associated with it by this time.[109] But they were apparently still conscious of the original decentralized agrarian structure of their older society as well. See, for example, the agricultural language applied to Israel in Psalm 80. An ecocritical reading of the books of Ezra and Nehemiah would give more clues in this respect, and to what extent the exile diminished the original agrarian identity.[110]

When the Romans dispersed the Jews for the last time in the first century AD, their religion was by necessity removed—until the twentieth-century—from the context that gave much of it expression and meaning. It would be like having transported tribes of North American plains Indians, like the Comanche or Blackfoot, to the lush fields of France or England—much of their religion would not have been able to express itself, it would have lost its context and therefore much of its literal meaning.

I will now move to the text of Proverbs, which holds much on these subjects.[*]

---

[*] See Appendix D for a brief history of agrarianism as seen through the lens of this study.

CHAPTER 5: THE BOOK OF PROVERBS

There are several impressions that are likely to strike the twenty-first century reader of Proverbs: the practical, applicable nature of the advice, the direct and simplistic nature of the form, the poetic rendering of many of the ideas—as well as the prominence of agricultural terms and situations.[111] Besides the frequency of proverbs relating actual agricultural situations we also find agricultural language even in proverbs dealing with royalty or the wealthy. A king "winnows out all evil with his eyes" (20.8), and he again "winnows out the wicked; he drives the threshing wheel over them" (20.26). This shows that the agricultural language of the people penetrated even to the urban circles of the educated. The question that this chapter will attempt to answer is to what extent not only rural language but rural values permeated the entire culture.

The sections of Proverbs break down as follows: section I "Prologue" (1.1-7), II "The Superiority of the Way of Wisdom" (1.8-9.18), III "The Proverbs of Solomon" (10.1-22.16), "Sayings of the Wise" IV (22.17-24-34), V "More Proverbs of Solomon" (25.1-29.27), VI "The Words of Agur and Lemuel" (30.1-31.9), and VII being an epilogue on a wife of noble character (31.10-31). But these section titles come from the editors of the NIV and do not do justice to the complexity within each section.[112]

Throughout the sections the proverbs bear a distinct parallel structure. The question here is less whether this represents a mnemonic device (it almost certainly does), but rather to what extent it reveals the way the ancient Hebrews saw reality. It is tempting to say that this demonstrates a mind that always saw things as right or wrong, good or bad. But a deeper look reveals that while certain proverbs demonstrate this, many others demonstrate more nuance and pragmatism than simple moral dualism. The parallelism indeed takes several forms: it can take the form of a) the same idea expressed in two slightly different ways, as in, "An angry man stirs up dissension, and a hot-tempered one commits many sins (29.22)";[113] it can take the form of b) comparison, as in, "As iron sharpens iron, so one man sharpens another (27.17)";[114] or it can take the form of c) contrast, as in "Evil men do not understand justice, but those who seek the Lord understand it fully (28.5)". Only this last evidences moral dualism—and so the overall way of looking at life is more saying that while certain situations are more clear-cut, many are more complex.[115]

The language of Proverbs shows a mixture of agricultural and informal influences on the one hand, and the poetic touch of urban and educated hands on the other—but the book is also composed of different collections, and is divided into distinct sections, with the agrarian nature of Hebrew society represented more in some sections than others.[116] Whybray asserts that the differences between the sections are related to the different social states of the speakers;[117] but he also says that although it is undisputable that sections IV and V for example originated as two different collections, there is still a remarkable consistency of viewpoint.[118] I will look later at Whybray's view of authorship, but it seems plausible because of this that the values and ethic of the proverbs came from the people, and the form of expression from educated urban editors.[119]

The language also bears the marks of the Hebrew conception of the relationship between man and the Divine. So for example, wisdom or morality is expressed as "the fear of the Lord" (1.7, 9.10, 31.30), and conversely the vicious person characterized as "an abomination to the Lord" (3.32, 6.16, 11.1). This is the language of Judaism.[120] Whybray says "the fear of the Lord" means, "obedience to the will of God made known through the religion of Israel."[121] But while this may be a strict definition of the phrase, he passes over one of the proverbs that defines it in more broad terms: "To fear the Lord is to hate evil;..." (8.13). In any case, the modes of expression in Proverbs are Judaic, but they are addressed to a more universal audience than the Law.[122] The word "Israel" for example does not occur once in the book of Proverbs, whereas the word for "man", *adam*, occurs thirty-three times.[123] Even today Proverbs would probably resonate more with non-Jews than other books in the Old Testament, although this universality may be a characteristic that most or all proverbs share. Also there is the possibility that this could be evidence of how the Hebrews editors gave a nod to a larger, pre-existing Near Eastern tradition of proverbs and wisdom literature.[124]

A thematic reference system across the sections shows the prominence of certain themes, and gives us a better idea of the most frequent topics. In my count, there are twelve passages that refer directly to agricultural situations.[125] There are five passages specifically referring to hunger.[126] There are seven passages that refer directly to work.[127] There are fifteen passages that deal explicitly with neighbors.[128] And there are twenty passages referring directly to wealth and poverty, the most of any single theme.[129] But it is difficult to decide which proverbs deserve inclusion in a particular list, because verses not referring explicitly to the presence of these social and economic situations may be using related language, or indirectly referring to other situations.

Whybray gives the following more inclusive counts: 120 of 513 verses refer to wealth, a comfortable existence, or positions of power and influence;[130] 103 out of 513 refer to a person being brought low by total disaster.[131] Just from these two sets of numbers we can see the social and economic reality of early Hebrew society coming into focus: life was a precarious agricultural struggle for subsistence, where wealth came slowly and was valued, and where hard work and good neighbors held real-life consequences. This evokes the environmental and social context of *Works and Days*.

Cohen calls the book's first major section, section II (1.8-9.18), a "preface", characterizing it as "a discourse on fundamentals".[132] The thrust of the message given here from a father to his son is more on the danger of moral folly and benefits of wisdom, and compared to the other sections agriculture does not hold a prominent place in it. But there is the important point that the young man the father is addressing is apparently a farmer. Proverbs 3. 9-10 reads, "Honor the Lord with your wealth, with the firstfruits of all your crops; then your barns will be filled to overflowing, and your vats will brim over with new wine." [133] Some scholars assert, however, that this passage is, again, wholly metaphorical, and that what we are dealing with here is an elderly Hebrew sage addressing a young aristocrat destined for a career in some official office.[134] In any case, what is more certain is that although work is not as conspicuous here as in other sections, 6.6-11 is perhaps the most representative and lengthy reference to the subject:

> Go to the ant, you sluggard, consider her ways and be wise! It has no commander, no overseer or ruler, yet it stores its provisions in summer and gathers its food at harvest. How long will you lie there, you sluggard? When will you get up from your sleep? A little sleep, a little slumber, a little folding of the hands to rest—and poverty will come on you like a bandit and scarcity like an armed man. (Prov. 6.6-11)

If this does not sound like Hesiod then what does? The valuing of hard work, the independence, the fear of poverty—all of these were alive and kicking in Greek culture during the Archaic period. In any case, of particular note in this passage is the reference to the ant having no overseer or ruler, which is commending the practices of an independent farmer over a situation where there are overseers. So while agriculture and work are not as proportionately dominant in this section, these passages show us the broader context.

Section III (10.1-22.16), which Cohen refers to the "main section of the book" contains proverbs strictly defined. The proverbs up to 15.20 evidence only examples of the third form, which contrast something positive with something negative; this shows that someone edited the collection. For the rest of the section each verse deals with one topic, paralleling in the various ways, although some verses do intermingle topics.

Sections IV (22.17-24.34) and V (25.1-29.27) give a prominent place to royal subjects, but agricultural language and particularly the subject of neighbors are still much in evidence.

Section VI (30.1-31.9) is a short section that has experienced much textual corruption.[135] This is not surprising in a book that has undergone much editing. 30.1 states that these words are the provenance of one Agur, who Whybray says may have been of north Arabian tribal origin.[136] In any case, the section is noteworthy here primarily for a passage articulating an eloquent espousal of middle class virtues:

> Two things I ask of you, O Lord; do not refuse me before I die: keep falsehood and lies far from me; give me neither poverty nor riches, but give me only my daily bread. Otherwise, I may have too much and disown you, and say, "Who is the Lord?" Or I may become poor and steal, and so dishonor the name of my God. (Prov. 30.7-9)

In relation to this study this passage speaks for itself.

Social justice also plays a conspicuous role in the book of Proverbs. The primary area that this comes out in is the repeated references to the rich taking advantage of the poor. We also saw this in Hesiod's fable. Specifically, widows, orphans, and aliens did not possess full civil rights in Israelite society, and therefore were open to exploitation.[137]

The Hebrew word for "work ethic" is *harûs,* which personified Whybray translates as "a hardworking person". The word occurs in no other book in the Old Testament, but five times in the book of Proverbs.[138]

Once again, despite the fact that the different sections show themselves to have originally been different collections, they have commonalities. We can see this in instances where a similar take on a concept is found in different sections: i.e. the mocker (9.7-9 & 23.9); the quarrelsome wife (21.9 & 25.24); adultery (7.1-27 & 23.26-28). And this is the case with agriculture as well (6-6-11, 24.30-34, 31.16). These instances would again argue that the rural and urban elements of ancient Hebrew society were in close contact and shared a common practical and sensible kind of ethic, and given the preponderance of the rural population, that this ethic was rural and agrarian. We also saw this urban knowledge of rural situations and values in Homer.

Proverbs evidences a preoccupation with adultery and other moral red herrings quite divorced from practical agricultural or other quotidian advice.[139] This is evidence of a particularly Hebrew emphasis, perhaps due to the presence of the Law and its stiff penalties (death) for such offences.[140]

But it must be said that the book's view of women does not tend to misogyny as does *Works and Days*. Proverbs personifies wisdom as a woman.[141] Also, the final section (VII) of the book, which is a sort of epilogue, states in a structural way what its first verse says outright: "A wife of noble character who can find? She is worth far more than rubies…" (31.10).

But what stands out most about this concluding passage is that the ideal woman is a full-fledged owner and manager of a farm: "She considers a field and buys it; out of her earning she plants a vineyard" (31.16). The mention of fields and vineyards portrays this as a diversified farm.[142] This scenario, which puts the emphasis on the role of women in this situation, reinforces what the entire book of Proverbs communicates so clearly—that the society from which these proverbs originated was a rural society of small freeholders, or an agrarian society.

CHAPTER 6: CRITICISM ON PROVERBS

For scholarship on Proverbs, Evan Eisenberg paints a broad background by giving information on important Old Testament scholars and relating works of historiography and ecocriticism. To begin this chapter it is simplest to quote directly his essay:

> In the first half of the twentieth century the German school of Alt and Noth predominated: this school denied the historicity of the Bible and spoke of gradual infiltration of Canaan by seminomadic tribes, which in time formed a loose confederation. About mid-century, a counterattack was led by William Foxwell Albright and the more radical Yehezkel Kaufmann, who propped up the patriarchal stories, and those of the conquest of Canaan, with shards and other evidence newly unearthed. In the last couple of decades the winds have shifted yet again, with William G. Dever, John van Seters, Norman K. Gottwalk, and George E. Mendenhall, among others, placing the Israelites more firmly in the a Canaanite context. (Mendenhall goes farthest, making the Israelites out to be downtrodden peasants of wholly native origin).[143]

See note for a list of other historiographical and ecocritical studies and further info.[144]

The two main questions of interest to this study on which scholars of Proverbs weigh in to varying degrees are: 1) which social group the proverbs came from, and 2) whether they express an agrarian philosophy and practice of daily life.

In respect to question 1), there apparently had been virtual consensus among scholars that Proverbs was the work solely of the upper classes. Again, as with Hesiod, the early scholarship was mostly German.[145] The main reasons for this assertion were due to the similarities of Proverbs to foreign (especially Egyptian) wisdom books whose backgrounds were royal courts,[146] and the attribution of the proverbs to Solomon (1.1, 10.1, 25.1; I Kings 4.32) and the "men of Hezekiah" (25.1).[147]

A few scholars, however, had long questioned this. In 1927, a German scholar already argued for the existence of a "middling class" of landowners (the *gibbôrê hayil*) who formed the basis of economic as well as military life in the pre-exilic period, but who were distinct from the governing class and no less subject to their oppressive policies than certain small peasants.[148] And a pre-eminent German scholar, Gerhard von Rad—whose *Theologie des Alten Testament I* (1957) Whybray calls "magisterial"—argued that section III was the product of a rural middle class.[149]

A. Cohen, a Jewish scholar, in his 1946 commentary, notes that Proverbs appears to be beyond the purview of religion, and relates the experiences of everyday life.[150] But he clarifies this statement by saying that, "no sharp dividing line exists in Judaism between the secular and the religious."[151] The same lack of division existed in Hesiod. He also clarifies the way in which the popular and educated influences combined to give us the proverbs as they are, saying that some of the proverbs were indeed folk sayings, but that they were not left in their original form and were elaborated into a poetical couplet for the purpose of heightening the force of the moral.[152] Cohen's is a good commentary, and lays out important issues with relation to Proverbs in a clear and concise manner.

Taking into consideration all the criticism on the question of authorship, this (Cohen's) is the conclusion most in line with the evidence. He does not deny the influence of educated persons in putting the sayings into the poetical form we now have, while acknowledging that the beliefs and ethic behind them came from the people.

Recent scholars are still split on question 1), although there seems to be more of a trend towards the conclusion of von Rad and Cohen. Obviously, if the proverbs show Egyptian or Mesopotamian influence, it is a blow to the contention of this study—that they bear the fingerprints of local small-scale agriculturalists. But that is apparently not the conclusion at which the majority of scholarship has eventually arrived.

R.N. Whybray is a scholar who has published several books on the book of Proverbs. He for his part seems to have changed his mind throughout the course of his academic career on this question (1). In his 1972 study he wrote, "It is difficult to avoid the conclusion that most of the sayings in Proverbs were literary creations whose authors had a high degree of education."[153] As evidence, he cited 1) the number of proverbs (i.e. that they were too numerous to be all popular sayings), and 2) that they are written poetically and strive for effect.[154] He said this assessment applies particularly to section II (ch.1-9), but also other sections.[155] At this point he was very strong on Proverbs being a product of educated circles heavily influenced by Egyptian precedents; he even said that the Hebrew practice of writing proverbs was transplanted from Egypt through Egyptian civil servants who helped Israel set up their national organization![156] He ascribed its teachings "of more general interest" to the progressive enlargement of the educated class in Israel during the course of its history,[157] and concluded that Proverbs had been written in scribal circles similar to those of Egypt and

Mesopotamia.[158] In his 1972 study Whybray did not give much attention a rural influence on the proverbs.

Taking this subject in hand, we know that the Hebrews were aware of the Mesopotamian and Egyptian wisdom traditions, and must have had some knowledge of their written works. I Kings 4:30-31 says, "Solomon's wisdom was greater than the wisdom of all the men of the East, and greater than all the wisdom of Egypt. He was wiser than any other man, including Ethan the Ezrahite—wiser than Heman, Calcol and Darda, the sons of Mahol..." But to say that the Hebrew practice of writing proverbs was transplanted from Egypt by Egyptian civil servants ignores the historical tension that existed between the Hebrews and Egyptians. References to the Hebrews in Egyptian records of any kind are scarce, and on the Hebrew side, the book of Judges does not mention the Egyptians once (except in reference to the Israelites having left there). Even after the change had been made toward centralization with the rise of the monarchical system at the outset of the United Kingdom period, there is no mention of Egypt in the historical books covering the period of the reigns of Saul and David (again except in reference to the past). In fact there is no contemporary reference to Egypt at all until the information on the reign of Solomon (I Kings 3.1). This is noteworthy. It argues that Egypt had a negligible influence on the philosophy behind, and the actual organization of the Hebrew's political and economic system up to that later point.

But by 1990 Whybray had apparently altered his opinion. In this study on wealth and poverty in Proverbs, he makes more of the distinctions between the sections, and argues that there is a different attitude between sections I, IV, and VII—and sections III and V. Here he says sections III and V are more representative of the people's traditional attitudes, and the others a different (assumedly urban and educated) one.[159] Let us recall that section III (10.1-22.16) is the "main" section of Proverbs, that it is the largest section in which the typical parallel proverb is found, and that throughout the sections wealth and poverty were the most frequent subjects to which the proverbs refer. By this time Whybray apparently had either changed his mind from his previous position or was simply putting more emphasis on the social and economic background instead of the composition or editing. In this study he concludes that,

> Such evidence as is to be found here suggests that their settings are predominantly those of small farmers farming their own land (and perhaps, to some extent, of an urban proletariat). It is strongly implied that only constant hard work allied with common sense and a resistance to the temptation to fritter away one's substance on

> inessentials and self-indulgence can stave off the threat of poverty…[160]

Once again this looks like the setting and work ethic in Hesiod. Whybray goes on:

> While some of the warnings would no doubt constitute sound advice if offered to members of any social class, they would undoubtedly be far more relevant to the circumstances of the manual worker than of the relatively secure upper class.[161]

It is significant here—as I emphasized with Hesiod—that Whybray sees manual labor as having been present. Here he is speaking specifically about section III. Whybray also notes that Leviticus is addressed to a rural farming community;[162] this supports the importance that I give the book in this study. He goes on to note the expression of middle-class attitudes in the passage 30.7-9,[163] and concludes, in contrast to his previous emphasis, that Proverbs is indeed the expression of a class of middling farmers.[164]

Whybray's reason for focusing here on this rural middle class is more because of his interest in class issues. His study touches on agrarianism, but does not go all the way in focusing on how the effects of this rural mindset branched out into other areas.

So besides Eisenberg and some of the studies that he references, there is not much ecocriticism that touches on Judges or Proverbs. More ecocritical analysis needs to be combined with what archaeological evidence we have for the pre-monarchic period to arrive at a scholarly consensus on the presence and nature of Hebrew agrarianism.

The teachings of the Judaic texts in regard to man's interaction with nature however are primarily important to us in the twenty-first century because of their influence on Christianity. This is not to disparage Judaism but to acknowledge that Christianity and the West are most implicated in the development of the modern world and the modern environmental crisis. Modern environmentalists are correct to search for something in Christianity that has soured the relationship between man and nature—but the critiques that I have read have always left me wanting.

I will attempt to advance my own critique in the next chapter.

CHAPTER 7: THE WESTERN VIEW OF NATURE

Archaic Greece was a formative period that gave rise to one of the world's most innovative civilizations. The Greeks created without precedent the arts as we know them, wrote and thought at levels that have rarely been attained since, and laid the culture of learning that took on Christianity and built Western and Byzantine civilizations.

But what the modern study of Greek learning has tended to forget is that the culture that produced Greek civilization was not urban but rural and agrarian. The early Greeks were predominantly small farmers who had to provide sustenance for their families as well as participate in the political and cultural life of the polis.

The Greek view of nature was therefore agricultural in the sense that it saw nature as something to be used within limits. There was a role for humans in the cosmos —the order of the world—and that role was to farm the land. On this the gods smiled.

But the Greeks were not unique in some respects. On the eastern shore of the Mediterranean there rose a land of hills not unlike the landscape of Greece. It was a land that flowed with milk and honey.

Early Hebrew culture too was rural and agrarian. During the Judges period there was no king and no central government at all. Defence was on an ad hoc basis and consisted on the yeomen gathering together to fight the enemies of Israel. Such expeditions and community life to some extent had a role for a "Judge"—a semi-religious semi-factotum figure like Samuel or Gideon—but that was all. The economy was agricultural and the unit of production the small farm. The religion of the Hebrews was tied intimately to the cycles of the agricultural calendar and the local landscape.

There was also apparently little thought in early Israel of a central urban focal-point. There is no injunction in the Law for such an organization, and the evidence from the other applicable Old Testament books indicates that for Israel's formative period Judaism originally functioned without such a centre. The city of Jerusalem did not rise to prominence until the reign of King David (c.1010-970 BC) circa three centuries after the Law and the entrance of the Israelites into the Levant, and in fact Jerusalem was not even primarily occupied by Jews before this later period.[165] The Temple for its part was not built until the reign of David's son Solomon (c.970-930 BC).

Altogether early Israel was perhaps the epitome of an agrarian society. We find the prescriptions for it in the Torah and the evidence that it was practiced in the Old Testament books of Joshua, Judges, Ruth, parts of the historical books, and in the broad social evidence in the book of Proverbs. I have detailed the latter in this study.

But there is one other textual reference that is central to the subject if this book. That is because it reinforces the agrarian philosophy of Leviticus and casts the book of Proverbs in its true light: that the proverbs are later historical proof that the agrarian philosophy of the Torah was actually practiced. This is perhaps the central verse, besides those of Leviticus 25, regarding the Hebrew view of nature:

> God blessed them and said to them, "Be fruitful and increase in number; fill the earth and subdue it. Rule over the fish of the sea and the birds of the air and over every living creature that moves on the ground." (Genesis 1.28)

The meanings of the pivotal verbs "subdue" (*kābaš*) and "rule" (*rādāh*)—to which critics of Judaism and Christianity's view of nature have drawn attention—imply seeing nature as something that human beings are to master forcibly.[166] And clearly they mean something along those lines. The other uses of the first verb in the Old Testament translate, "to subject, force, keep under, bring into bondage",[167] and the second verb is also a forceful word.[168] There is therefore little doubt about the meaning of these verbs.

But Wendell Berry has pointed out that scholars in the past have draw distinctions regarding the object of *kābaš* here. He notes that the Oxford Dictionary gives one of the definitions of "to subdue" as "*to bring (land) under cultivation*", and that in illustration of this meaning the editors cite the Coverdale translation of this very verse in Genesis! Berry also mentions that this is how Pope understood this verse.[169]

To state the obvious: to put land under cultivation is a significantly different injunction than subduing all of the elements and forces of nature to serve human ends. Agriculture can only be practiced on a small part of the earth's surface, it has limits, and it demands sustainability and nurture if it is to continue. And farmers of the tough Mediterranean highlands would have understood all the more clearly that these were the connotations that this commission implied. Also I want to recall here that while Genesis 1:28 comes from the first Creation account in Genesis, Genesis 3:17-19 in the second account gives a similar injunction to cultivate the earth.[170]

Overall these verses in Genesis are astonishing in light of the evidence from Proverbs that proves the Hebrew view of nature was agrarian, and not rapacious. It all leads to the conclusion that Judaism is not necessarily inimical to the natural world.

But Judaism is certainly not Christianity. While the latter interpreted and borrowed much from the former there are differences as well. I will move on to Christianity by looking first at the New Testament to see the extent to which the agrarian ethic of the Old Testament is present there.

It is my opinion that the agrarian ethic of Judaism did survive to some extent right up to time of Jesus and the Apostles. First of all we see that the original economic infrastructure and philosophy were consciously continued throughout the centuries in Israel by evidence from numerous examples in the later books of the Old Testament. Agriculture is prominent in the book of Ruth, which relates a story from the Judges period; around three hundred years later, the prophet Elisha is still portrayed plowing his own fields with his own oxen when Elijah comes to call him to be his successor (I Kings 19.20). And apparently the Jewish economic philosophy was still tied up with small independent farming even after the disturbances brought about by the Roman conquest of Judea. The continuance of the economic practice of the Jewish religion can be seen to have survived right up to the time of Jesus in the first century AD by his ubiquitous use of agricultural language and metaphors involving small scale privately owned land: the parable of the sower (Mark 4), the parable of the weeds (Matthew 13), the parable of the vineyard (Matthew 20) etc… This habit in the language of Jesus is most likely due to having grown up in small-town Judea, but also may be because as a Jew he was familiar with the Old Testament. In any case, the agrarian outlook is still in evidence.

The Jewish custom of having to have a trade also must be recalled here. It was customary that every respectable Jew in the first century AD had to teach his son a trade of some kind.[171] For instance, even the erudite St. Paul saw no shame in working as a tent-maker (Acts 18.3). In a passage in which he writes about this explicitly he says, "Make it your ambition to lead a quite life, to mind your own business and to work with your hands, just as we told you, so that your daily life may win the respect of outsiders and so that you will not be dependent on anybody (I Thessalonians 4:11)." This sounds like the work ethic of Proverbs. Jesus worked as a carpenter, and most of the Apostles were fishermen. So with Jesus, the Apostles, and St. Paul all exhibiting this ethic there is enough evidence to identify this as the early Christian view with regards to physical work and the body.

But what happened to the agrarian traditions of Judaism after the time of Jesus? In other words *to what extent did later Christianity perpetuate the agrarian ethic of Judaism? And if so how did it do this and how did it cease doing this?*

In my view these questions start to get at the real issues with respect to what has gone wrong with the modern world and the environment. They require, however, knowledge of specific times and places during the medieval or modern periods, and as I am not a specialist in either I cannot enter into them fully here (see Montmarquet).

I do think it is safe to say, however, that Judaic agrarianism never took hold in Western Christianity—and I will offer several explanations for this from the period of the early Church, a period with which I am more familiar.[172]

First of all, both Western and Eastern (Orthodox) Christianity have always had a shaky relationship with the Jews, whose religious leaders crucified Jesus and harried the early Jewish and Gentile converts to Christianity. But Christians more than evened the score—and for pretty much the rest of the story the persecuting has been going the other way since the fourth century AD and the conversion of Constantine. In any case, there has always been a parallel tension in much of Christian theology and teaching as to what to do with the plethora of minutely specific laws in the Old Testament.

It was the view of St. Paul, who had been a strict adherent to the Jewish code, that the Law had been there to point to the inability of human beings to be justified before God based on legalism (Romans 4) and that Jesus had ushered in a new era in which God lived within human beings through faith (Romans 9; Hebrews 10,11). Because of this the different branches of Christianity have held to not applying literally the instructions of the Torah. But most have also held that the God of the Old Testament is the God of the New, and that the essence, or philosophy of the Law is still in effect. Jesus claimed that this essence was love, summed up in his "So in everything, do to others what you would have them do to you, for this sums up the Law and the Prophets" (Matthew 7.12).

But other of the statements of Jesus and St. Paul with respect to the Law appear contradictory and have undoubtedly caused confusion on the subject. Jesus says elsewhere, "Do not think I that I have come to abolish the Law or the Prophets; I have not come to abolish them but to fulfill them. I tell you the truth, until heaven and earth disappear, not the smallest letter, not the least stroke of a pen, will by any means disappear from the Law until everything is accomplished" (Matthew 5.17-18). St. Paul reiterates this adamantly, "Do we, then, nullify the law by this faith? Not at all! Rather, we uphold the law." (Romans 3.31). He then goes on to advance how Abraham lived the essence of the Law, but he does not get into economics and does not mention Leviticus 25.

So I advance that the Christian tension with regard to the Jews and uncertainty with respect to the Law may have contributed to causing the economic *essence* of the Law to have been sidelined and forgotten in at least Western Christianity.

A second reason that the early Church may have been reluctant to focus on the economic elements of Judaism is because of its program to stamp out the vestiges of paganism, which was stronger in typically conservative, rural areas. Christianity was perforce more of an urban religion in its early stages because the itinerant teachers that spread it, as in St. Paul, naturally went first to the synagogues and agorae of the urban centres; the book of Acts and the Epistles (which are addressed to urban churches) are evidence of this. So it is not surprising that Christianity seems to have been reluctant to focus on the agrarian elements of Judaism, and likewise not to have given a more prominent place to similar elements in the Greco-Roman tradition (i.e. Hesiod, Virgil's *Georgics* etc…).

Thirdly, the early Christians did not hold political power until the fourth century. Before that point, to have attempted to deal with the agricultural issues of the Roman Empire (which were also social and economic issues) was beyond their power, and they probably did not think of it as either possible or advisable. These issues in Italy had reached a climax as far back as the second century BC with Tiberius and Gaius Gracchus, whose reforms had attempted to address the growth of larger estates worked by slave-labour and the dispossession of the original small Roman land-holders (for more on this important period in Roman history see Appendix A). The reforms did not alter the course of events and the Later Roman Empire saw the dominance of the Latifundiae—the large agricultural estates of the slave-owning aristocracy. Therefore it would have been a bold Christian indeed who would have drawn attention with any seriousness to the land-owning yeomen of the Jewish Scriptures. The early Church fathers instead focused on establishing the theological doctrine of the new religion. And when Constantine and later Christian Roman Emperors rose to power, Judaism had been a religion divorced from its context for several hundred years and in their own history the Gracchi too were part of the distant past. Either they simply forgot about these elements or for some other reason they just never rose to prominence.

It is a complicated subject but all these factors add up to explain to some extent why the tradition of Judaic agrarianism does not appear to have taken hold in Western Christianity.[173]

But I also raise two other explanations for the lack of Judaic agrarianism within Western Christianity. There is also the argument that the Church did retain the basic Judaic view of nature to a large degree throughout the Middle Ages—albeit in a more Homeric than Hesiodic or

Judaic social structure—and that it is only in the modern era that it has left it behind.[174] This deals with the questions that I stressed earlier.

And lastly, there is the influence of Platonic philosophy upon Christianity. I will look more closely at this a little later on.

*****

I advanced previously that the New Testament evidences the agrarian outlook of Judaism and insinuated in so doing that Christianity is not necessarily inimical to the natural world. But different modern writers and academics have concluded otherwise.

Historian Lynn White Jr. published his seminal essay "Historical Roots of Our Ecological Crisis" over forty years ago,[175] but his arguments still raise the issues and therefore provide a good base from which to discuss the Christian view of nature.[*]

In his essay White Jr. censures Christianity for being what he sees as anthropocentric,[176] and its view of nature for having produced the modern science and technology that have caused the crisis.[177]

In my opinion White Jr. in his first assertion does not show the nuances that make up anthropocentrism, but in my view with his second assertion he has a much better argument.

The main problem with White Jr.'s first point is that how is it possible for us not to be anthropocentric? Thinking takes place within our heads, and action through our bodies, and so it is literally impossible for human beings to be exo-ontological or non-anthropocentric.

Granted, the American Heritage Dictionary does define "anthropocentric" as, "Interpreting reality in terms of human values and experience." So if what White Jr. and others are saying is that humans need to be more empathetic to other matter and life—to put themselves in context and act on the basis that nature is not there *just* to serve them—then their argument is reasonable and valid. But this is still anthropocentrism. It is essentially a more balanced anthropocentrism—because we cannot escape anthropocentrism any more than we can our own bodies and minds.

Furthermore, if the problem in environmental discourse is how to define the term "anthropocentrism", then we should skip employing this word and keep focusing on more basic ones like greed, arrogance, and/or selfishness—because anthropocentrism is not only inescapable but necessary for civil society. The first concern of human beings living in community is

---

[*] Please see Appendix E for a brief statement on the state of ecocriticism now.

to co-exist and subsist, and this calls for social, political, and economic organization—it requires paying the most attention to the functioning of the human community. This does not mean once again, that there cannot and should not be a place for other creatures and matter and that to infringe upon that is equally as disruptive as putting other creatures in the place of humans. But it still requires anthropocentrism. Also if a religion were not anthropocentric it would be irrelevant to much of human life such as personal relationships and one's role in a community. Therefore it is not a bad thing that a society or religion be anthropocentric as long as they maintain a proper view and place for other creatures and parts of nature. And these arguments apply to all societies and their religions.

And so if the "anthropocentric" argument against Christianity is the one under discussion, the real issue is that of civilization being tied to agriculture as opposed to the impossibility of its existence in a state of wild nature. This is a point that is lost upon much public and environmental discourse.[178] Old Testament Israel and New Testament Judea, like all settled societies including those of Western Europe, necessarily practiced agriculture and the domestication of animals, so it is understandable that there should be more focus on agriculture and shepherding in the Old and New Testaments. They, like all mixed agricultural and bucolic economies, certainly did tend to see wild nature as the antagonist. And the same dynamic still exists today in rural localities around the world. But this only makes sense if a bear or lion is living around the bend and remaining obstinate in the exercise of a predilection for eating members of your family or flock. It is only in an urbanized environment that a bear or lion can procure a more endearing reputation. This can stray, undoubtedly, into disrespecting and exterminating wild nature—but only if taken to the extreme. I would say that the extreme is the incursion of habitat and the wiping out of species; but this is not what is enjoined in the limited injunction of Genesis 1.28. What is urged there is to bring arable land under cultivation, and agriculture is only possible on a certain amount of an ecosystem's land. So unless a purposeful campaign of extermination is undertaken then there will always be a place in an agricultural society for wild nature. A germane example of this in ancient times is the presence of large carnivores—bears and lions— around Bethlehem in the time of David (I Samuel 17.36). And large carnivores are present in Israel throughout the Old Testament (I Kings 13.34; 20.36; II Kings 17.25).[179] That wild nature and agriculture can co-exist on those parts of an ecosystem's land to which each is suited was also the case in both Chinese and Indian civilizations until recent industrialization and commercialization. Otherwise the panda bear would have been extinct several millennia ago and English nobles would not have had any tigers to hunt. If humans will occupy themselves in their realm—then wild animals will survive just fine on their own.

My response to White Jr.'s first point then is that civilization cannot help but be anthropocentric, that this is not necessarily antithetical to ecology, and that in theory, if it were to be true to its own Scriptures and certain of its intellectual traditions, Christianity should be agrarian. But theory is not practice, which brings us to his second point—that modern science and technology are a product of Christian natural theology.

In my view White Jr. has a point that the Christian view of nature produced modern science and technology in two respects.

First off all I think that White Jr. has an argument within the limits of the agrarian worldview (although I don't think that this is what he was referring to and so I agree partially with him). In his own words White Jr. says:

> We would seem to be headed toward conclusions unpalatable to many Christians. Since both *science* and *technology* are blessed words in our contemporary vocabulary, some may be happy at the notions, first, that, viewed historically, modern science is an extrapolation of natural (Christian-NM) theology, and second, that modern technology is at least partly to be explained as an Occidental, voluntarist realization of the Christian dogma of man's transcendence of, and rightful mastery over, nature."[180]

But the transcendence of humanity over nature that we see in Genesis 1:28 must be put in the context of both the verse itself (which says that humanity is to engage in agriculture) and that of the culture of the author of the verse, which was certainly agricultural and in which any mastery over nature was confined to what was then conceivable. Therefore there is a case for Genesis 1:28 enjoining technology that would further agrarianism—but not for commissioning technology that would serve a purpose beyond its limits.

I grant, however, that if there is room for extra-agricultural transcendence it is in the second part of the pivotal verse—where the earth is not mentioned and humans are told: "Rule over the fish of the sea and the birds of the air and over every living creature that moves on the ground." And yet I suggest that even this may be referring to the domestication of animals. I do this first because the first part of the verse commissioned agriculture, and second because it would explain the connotations of Near Eastern kingship in *Rdh*.[181] The harsh meanings of *Rdh* make sense in the context of domesticating animals.

It is also important to note that science and technology as we know them are not prominent in the Bible and I can say with reason that they are for all intents and purposes non-existent. Any extrapolation that White Jr. or anyone else may make comes from the basic Judaic or Christian views of nature or "natural theology", primarily of Genesis 1:28. But I have raised that that pivotal verse inserts the agrarian element of limits.

Secondly I think that White Jr. has an argument that the Judeo-Christian dogma of creation gave science and technology impetus to the extent that later Christianity differs from early, New Testament Christianity. What I am referring to here specifically is the extent to which later Christianity took on the ontology of Plato.

Let us first consider Plato's ontology. Plato's basic view of reality is that there is the metaphysical realm and the physical realm, and that the former is superior to the latter (*Republic* 509D–510b; *Parmenides* 135d-135e). Furthermore, he applies this hierarchy to the soul and body (*Republic* 380d-381c).

And the New Testament parallels Plato to a certain extent. The Gospel of John says, "In the beginning was the Word (ὁ λόγοσ), and the Word was with God, and the Word was God. He was with God in the beginning." (John 1:1-2) Moreover Jesus insinuates something similar to Plato's hierarchy when he admonishes people to store up their treasures in heaven "where moth and rust do not destroy." (Matthew 6:19-21)

But there is a definite point of divergence here at which the New Testament goes one way and Plato the other. There is basically more balance in the New Testament between the metaphysical and the physical and specifically between the human body and soul. While the New Testament places value in the soul, I detailed earlier how it retains the Judaic conception of physical work. Furthermore, the whole idea of the messiah—God taking physical form—is the absolute opposite of Plato's idea. The passage in John goes on, "The Word became flesh and made his dwelling among us." (John 1:14)

Therefore it is easy to ascribe some of the theoretical motivations of modern science and technology to Christianity when in fact it is more accurate to attribute them to Plato. I have brought forward in this book that we cannot attribute the theoretical motivation behind the adoption of modern technology in the instance of agriculture to early Greek culture, Roman culture, Judaism, or New Testament Christianity. I believe that in this instance we should ascribe it to Plato.[182]

So in response to Whyte Jr.'s second point I argue that the degree to which we can attribute the driving force behind modern technology in particular to Christianity is the degree to which it adopted Plato's ontology and view of the body. It was the Platonic elements within Christianity that gave modern science and technology impetus and not Judaic natural theology.

CHAPTER 8: CONCLUSION

In the preceding chapter I took my assertion that the early Greeks and the early Hebrews were agrarian and proceeded to discuss the Christian view of nature. My discussion of this subject has touched on anthropocentrism and the element that modern science and technology are products of Christian natural theology.

I conclude that Christianity is indeed anthropocentric but that this is not necessarily incompatible with ecology. I advance also that Christianity is implicated in the development of modern science and technology, but that these developments did not arise out of its own natural theology, but its adoption of certain Greek thinking.

APPENDIX A

The word "agrarian" entered English through reference to the *lex sempronia agraria* of Tiberius Gracchus, who held the Roman office of tribune in 133 BC. A tribune was the representative on the plebeian class who held important powers in the Roman system of legislative assemblies.[183] This law was an attempt to redistribute land to free Roman citizens that had been gobbled up by large landholders who worked their estates with slaves. The confiscatory element of it proved very provocative to those who benefited under the system as it had been allowed to develop. Tiberius and later his brother Gaius were killed in serious civil strife that ensued.[184]

Therefore the term "agrarian" in English originally held revolutionary connotations. This meaning is implied, for example, in James Harrington's use of the word "agrarian" in *Commonwealth of Oceana* (1656). In the late eighteenth century, Thomas Jefferson and James Madison still continued to associate the word with economic and social leveling, specifically the equalization of ownership of cultivated land.[185] And yet while the term was more controversial in English than other European languages, "agrarian" in English also has had other less controversial definitions. In Jefferson's time a second use referred simply to the somewhat equal division of land (not imposed but simply describing a situation where this was the case); this is the definition given to it in Noah Webster's first American dictionary in 1806.[186] A third meaning follows other European languages in referring most generally to "cultivated land". Govan says that *agrarisch* in German and *agrarien* in French most frequently have meant simply "agricultural".[187] This study notes however that the adjective *agraire* in French contains the redistributive connotations. John Adams and Jefferson also used it in certain instances in the most general sense.[188]

The number of and variation among the definitions betrays the nebulous use of the word in English. Govan says that the word has been used "almost existentially" in various historical periods.[189] In Jefferson's time it held socialistic connotations, and later on to the Grangers in the post Civil-War United States it evoked communism.[190]

It was in the publication of *I'll Take My Stand* in 1930 that the term underwent an almost complete reversal, there referring to an agricultural philosophy of life in the tradition of Jefferson and the South opposed to industrialism. The use of this word in the introduction of *I'll Take My Stand* is an interesting choice that in historical perspective shows itself to have been a turning point in the English etymology of the term.

The Twelve Southerners were certainly aware of the history of the word, and although evidencing significant variation from one to the other, all assented to its use in the common statement of principle that is John Crow Ransom's introduction. And so their use of it was probably a savvy bit of semantic manipulation. The Northern press of the time would have labeled outright the treatise as a hopelessly outdated bit of nostalgia if the Southern authors had simply chosen to use terms like "rural life" or "farm life" to describe what they were defending. Even with the overtly communistic term "agrarian" the book was thus labeled. So their choice of the word probably was a preemptive effort at thwarting such a characterization. The Vanderbilt Agrarians were a combination of Classical liberals and conservatives with an agrarian frame of mind who were defending the rural culture of the South (varying amongst themselves in defending the manifestation of this in its aristocracy or yeomanry), and attempted to craft the presentation of their views to circumvent the calumny of influential segments of the academia and press of the time. In relation to present day realities, the book deserves attention in contemporary environmental dialogue for its insights into and prognostications concerning industrialism.

But since the advent of the environmental movement in the 1970s, the term "agrarian" in English has undergone another significant change. It is safe to say that compared to the attempt to induce a rebirth of it in *I'll Take My Stand* it is now enjoying a marked renaissance. This represents however the eventual success of the Twelve Southerners in the sense that it is now, as they attempted to do then, associated with a contemporary, forward looking philosophy.

Since the 1970's the term in literary, academic, and (to what extent it comes up in popular discourse) has lost all of its originally negative revolutionary or communistic evocations, as well as any opprobrious connections with Southern racism, and has now come to be associated more with a defense of rural life in the face of industrial agriculture, and a forward looking environmental activism.

The new aura having been cast upon the term is thanks in a large part to the writings of Wendell Berry, and his paradoxical place amongst the pantheon of the environmental movement in North America and the UK. Besides his many books of fiction, poetry, and non-fiction (Berry is perhaps best known as an essayist) Berry writes for such environmental beacons as *Orion* magazine in the United States, and *Resurgence* in the UK. He admits having taken much from the authors of *I'll Take My Stand*, but is quick to distance himself from the racist beliefs of the extreme members of the group.[191] Berry asserts that African Americans in the South learned the knowledge of the land better than most whites, but he is also sensitive to the effects of slavery on the psyches of both communities.[192] Berry's use of "agrarian" retains social and political elements but puts a greater emphasis, unlike the Twelve Southerners, on the environmental benefits of it as a practical economic system. He submits to the description of an "agrarian writer", using "we agrarians" to describe those in this wing of the environmental movement.[193] Obviously, Berry is a respected forerunner to some of the central contentions of this study, although in this study I have gone into ancient history to locate the origins of the yeoman type, and to see how Western civilization became separated from his mindset.

Although all of these attempts to define agrarianism need to be time and place specific, there are certain continuous elements to the term that span historical examples. These elements may not have always been called "agrarian", and as we have seen the word has indeed meant very different things—but the ideas have always been around.

Because of this I advance that if an author uses the word agrarian today it must necessarily contain a few of these connotations. This is not a subjective proclamation but an opinion based on how authors most often now use the word. Firstly, if an author uses the word agrarianism today it should contain the connotation that farming is a particularly valuable occupation to society. Montmarquet raises this point, that the essential aspect in which "agrarian" now differs from "agricultural" in that the former includes the assertion that agriculture is an especially important and valuable force in society.[194] It would be helpful to the environmental movement if the term also continued to increase in its association with the ecological agriculture that Berry advocates. There is no way of getting around that the term still represents a complex philosophy, and while not taking away from its intellectual heritage, I grant that it is more a "way of life" than any narrowly defined part of life. But there is no reason why it cannot retain its broadness while still having prominent, specific aspects.

In conclusion here, this environmental use of the term, with a still prominent but secondary place for social, political, and economic aspects, is the direction in which the use of the term agrarian is moving.

APPENDIX B

An essential distinction between periods and specific historical examples is the distinction between aristocratic agrarianism and agrarianism amongst the yeomanry. Aristocratic agrarianism functions in more of an estate system, where the owner does not do his own work i.e. Xenophon, Cato the Elder. In the agrarianism of the middle-class on the other hand the owner works his own land. He may hire others as well but he is not solely the owner, or overseer or manager.

An aristocracy existed in Greece in the Archaic period according to Jaeger, but the consensus is that yeomen were then preponderant (large-scale land ownership seems to have been anathema in early Israel). And yet the former shared certain key concepts with the latter. Xenophon's *Oeconomicus* gives us evidence for this.

In terms of their views of nature the differences between the two are negligible. Both saw nature as something to be used within limits. Both saw agriculture as having a privileged place among occupations. Such similarities are perhaps why Aristophanes made distinctions more between rural and urban Greece than within rural Greece.

APPENDIX C

The word ἀγρόσ (Latin AGER) in the singular refers to "a farm, an estate" (Od. XXIV.205). Although it occurs most often in the plural meaning "fields, lands" (Il. 23.832; Od.4.757; Pindar P. 4.265). It can also mean "the country" in general as opposed to the city.[195] An adjectival derivative is ἀγροικοσ; this could indicate "of the country",[196] or could produce a negative evocation along the lines of "clownish, boorish, rude, rough, course"; Plato uses repeatedly this and related words in the second sense.[197] Aristophanes uses these words ironically to mock urban pretension.[198] This word game informs us that there existed in Greece an urban/rural dynamic similar to the modern.

This study suggests that the noun in the Greek language closest to representing the idea or philosophy of agrarianism would probably have been οἰκονομία. That this is justified is indicated firstly in the multiple words Liddell and Scott ascribe to it; they translate it as all three: "the management of a household or family, husbandry, thrift". If the only rendering given was "the management of a household" then it could not represent the term agrarianism in English because there is no sense of a connection with the natural world. But we see in fact that in this translation the economic management aspect combines with something having to do with the natural world (husbandry). That is why I argue here that οἰκονομία is the closest Greek word to what agrarianism has become in contemporary English.

But did οἰκονομία carry the intellectual connotations of agrarianism? Clearly, in the time of Hesiod in the eighth century BC, the ideas he entrusted to writing were still more a "way of life" than a systematic body of thought. But by the time of Xenophon's *Oeconomicus* in the fifth century, the ideas first found in Hesiod had coalesced into what can be identified as more of a philosophy. The author is not read enough in philosophy to be authoritative on this point, but I know that for a body of thought to be classified as a philosophy it traditionally had to be more of a system of thought. And Xenophon's choice of the word οἰκονομία to entitle his treatise argues along these lines; and even if someone else later thus entitled the work this still applies. In light of this it is not strange that we see Xenophon reasserting this in the text, where he has his upper class Athenian "farmer" Ischomachus discussing agrarian subjects with Socrates while lounging on the steps of a temple as would philosophers of any school.[199] Aristotle furthermore also wrote a treatise entitled Τὰ Οἰκονομικά (although here it means more "those who are thrifty, frugal, economical"). Also, it is important to recall that because the economy of ancient Greece in all periods was dominantly agricultural, these terms and related issues were not esoteric or marginal subjects.

See note for examples of the use of οἰκονομία and cognate words in other works.[200]

A general term something along the lines of our "worker" that was applied to those doing agricultural work was ἐργάτησ.[201] And more generally οὑργάτησ λεώσ "the country-folk" (Aristophanes *Pax* 632).

We then have γεωργόσ, literally "earth-worker"; Liddell and Scott translate it as "husbandman", "small land-owner".[202] They are referred to as a group as γεωργόσ ὄχλοσ (Dionysus Halicarnassus 10.53). They are opposed to οἱ μισθαρνοῦωτεσ, "wage-earners" (Arist.Pol.4.12,3), and to ὁ δεσπότησ τοῦ χωρίου, (Corpus Inscriptionem 355.21), which would be referring to the master or lord of a larger estate.

Also αὐτουργόσ (Eur. Or. 920; Plat. Rep. 505A), which Liddell and Scott define as "husbandman", "poor farmer". αὐτουργόσ is differentiated from γεωργόσ in that the former was the word for one who works his own land without slaves.[203]

APPENDIX D

The following is a very brief history of agrarianism as seen through the lens of this study, which will hopefully at least begin to fill in some of the gaps that have to exist in such an undertaking that tries to bridge ancient history and modern issues.[204]

In terms of having gone farthest in agrarian ideas in literary and intellectual avenues, Greece lays the greatest claim. This is proven in that Virgil used Hesiod as his blueprint for the *Georgics* and Theocritus for the *Eclogues* and not (if there were to have been such Greek writers after Virgil) the other way around. In the Greek context, Hesiod laid the foundation and Xenophon chiseled the capstone.

But of course Virgil also had his own tradition behind him. I don't want to diminish Roman agrarianism or the paramount influence of Roman culture on especially Western Christianity; it is simply that I cannot enter into it here. It is beyond doubt that agrarianism was also prominent in Roman history and that there is profound depth that Roman history adds to the term and ideas behind it. In what way Roman agrarianism differed from the Greek and Hebrew and how it impacted subsequent interaction of Western civilization with the natural world is a subject worthy of exclusive study.

That οἰκονομία in the Greek context contained reference to not only the household but larger societal spheres was well developed in the Greek world by Xenophon's time. There are many references in the *Oeconomicus* to the household and the running a farm as being the state in microcosm (that a diversified farm is the larger economy in microcosm forms another large subject). In any case, no substantial innovations in this system of thought occurred after Xenophon in the Greek world of which I am aware.

An interesting point that I will raise here with respect to Western Europe in the Middle Ages (particularly the different monastic communities) is to what extent did it get its ideas of agriculture from the Judaic strand of agrarianism or from the Classical?

The modern period saw varying instances of a revival of Classical agrarianism because of the renewed influence in classical models after the Renaissance. Once again, to get into these large subjects in even close to sufficient detail is not possible here, and I plead relief and reference to Montmarquet.

In answer to the previous question, one thing in my view that is conspicuous is that scholars have not given the influence of the Judaic strand of agrarian thought both before and after the Renaissance enough attention.

I have argued that the strand of Judaic agrarianism was never prominent within Western Christianity—but certain Christians have always been aware of it. This study defers to Medievalists for comment on that period. As for the modern era, the dominant modern agrarians certainly took their ideas primarily from the Classical models. For example, the Physiocrats of eighteenth century France believed agriculture was the source of all true wealth, and that the laws of the state should restrain commerce and industry, which bears close resemblance to the Roman model, and does not show the influence of Judaism or Christianity.[205] Thomas Jefferson likewise transmuted his agrarian ideas from the texts of the Classical era, and not Genesis 1.28, Leviticus, Joshua, Judges, or Proverbs. But other modern authors and the movements in which they have been involved show more Christian influence. G.K. Chesterton is a prominent example of this as well as Wendell Berry.

APPENDIX E

The rise of ecocriticism is an encouraging trend. This study contends that looking at agrarianism in certain texts is a part of this but is a new development as well. The difference between ecocriticism and "agrarian analysis" is that the latter looks at the theory of agriculture and its interaction with the environment in a work of literature. Ecocriticism is the prerequisite for agrarian analysis, because to understand the relationship of agriculture to the natural world in a given text we still need to have determined what the relationship to nature is in that instance (if it is "agrarian").

I have used White Jr.'s essay as a jumping point in this study but I want to stress that I believe that the debate has moved on in significant ways. It is now pretty much accepted that that there is a problem and that that problem originated with the West and Christianity (although I reserve with the Platonic influence on Christianity). Wendell Berry's views on agriculture also are becoming more orthodox.[206] Therefore the debate now is the future of economics (of the global economy and of national and local economies) and the relationship between industrial technology and agriculture.

WORKS CITED

Berry, Wendell. *A Continuous Harmony*. 1970, 1972; Washington D.C.: Shoemaker and Hoard, 2003.
--- *Standing by Words*. 1983; Washington DC: Shoemaker and Hoard, 2005.
Bintliff, J.L. & A.M. Snodgrass. "The Cambridge/Bradford Boeotian Expedition: The First Four Years." *Journal of Field Archaelogy* 12:123-61.
Cohen, A. *Proverbs*. 1946; London, Jerusalem, New York: The Soncino Press, 1985.
Cohen, Jeremy. *"Be Fertile and Increase, Fill the Earth and Master It": The Ancient and Medieval Career of a Biblical Text*. Ithaca: Cornell University Press, 1989.
De Tocqueville, Alexis. *De la Démocratie en Amérique I, & II*. Édition Gallimard, 1961.
Drabble (ed.). *The Oxford Companion to English Literature*, 1985.
Edwards, Anthony T. *Hesiod's Ascra*. University of California Press, 2004.
Evelyn-White, Hugh G. *Hesiod: Homeric Hymns, Epic Cycle, Homerica*. 1914; Cambridge, Mass. & London: Loeb Classical Library, 1998.
Fränkel, Hermann. *Early Greek Poetry and Philosophy*. Ger. orig. 1962; trans. by Moses Hadas & James Willis; New York & London: Harcourt Brace Jovanovich,1973.
Freeman, Charles. *Egypt, Greece, and Rome: Civilizations of the Ancient Mediterranean*. Oxford: Oxford University Press, 1996.
Gaspar, Joseph W. *Social Ideas in the Wisdom Literature of the Old Testament*. Washington DC: The Catholic University of America Press, 1947.
Glotfelty, Cheryl and Fromm, Harold. *The Ecocriticism Reader: Landmarks of Literary Ecology*. Athens & London, the University of Georgia Press, 1996.
Hanson, Victor Davis. *The Other Greeks: the Family Farm and the Agrarian Roots of Western Civilization*. New York: The Free Press, 1995.
Hornblower, Simon & Antony Spawforth (eds.). *The Oxford Classical Dictionary* (3rd ed. rev.). Oxford: Oxford University Press, 2003.
Jaeger, Werner. *Paideia: the Ideals of Greek Culture*. In Three Volumes. Trans. By Gilbert Highet. New York: Oxford University Press, 1945.
Liddell, Henry George & Scott, Robert. *Greek-English Lexicon, Eighth Ed.* New York, Chicago, Cincinnati: American Book Company, 1897.
Leitch, Vincent B. (ed.). *The Norton Anthology of Theory and Criticism*. New York & London: W.W. Norton & Company, 2001.

Mazon, Paul. "Hésiode: La Composition des *Travaux et des jours.*" *Revue des Études Anciennes* 14 (1912) : 328-55.
--------. *Les Travaux et les Jours.* Paris : Hachette, 1914.
Millett, Paul. "Hesiod and his World." *Cambridge Philological Society Proceedings* 209 (1984) 84-115.
Montmarquet James A.. *The Idea of Agrarianism.* Moscow, Idaho: University of Idaho Press, 1989.
Morris, Ian. *Archaeology as Cultural History. Words and Things in Iron Age Greece.* Oxford, 2000.
Nelson, N. *Medieval Agrarian Economy.* New York: Henry Holt & Company, 1936.
Nelson, Stephanie A. *God and the Land: the Metaphysics of Farming in Hesiod and Virgil.* Oxford & New York: Oxford University Press, 1998.
Osborne, Robin. *Greece in the Making.* London & New York: Routledge, 1996.
Redfield, Robert. *The Primitive World and its Transformations.* Ithaca: Cornell University Press, 1953.
Reverdin O. (ed.). *Hésiode et son Influence.* Fondation Hardt, vol.7. Geneva: Fond. Hardt, 1962.
Smith, Kimberly K.. *Wendell Berry and the Agrarian Tradition.* University of Kansas Press, 2003.
Solmsen, Friedrich. *Hesiod and Aeschylus.* Cornell University Press, 1949..
Starr, Chester. *The Economic and Social Growth of Greece 800-500 B.C.* Oxford: Oxford University Press, 1977.
Stockton, David. *The Gracchi.* Oxford: Clarendon Press, 1979.
------. *The Classical Athenian Democracy.* New York & Oxford: Oxford University Press, 1990.
The American Heritage Dictionary, Fourth Ed.. New York: A Dell Book, 2001.
Tandy David W. & Neale Walter C. *Hesiod's Works and Days: A Translation and Commentary for the Social Sciences.* Berkeley: University of California Press, 1996.
Tirosh-Samuelson, Hava (ed.). *Judaism and Ecology: Created World and Revealed Word.* Cambridge, Massachusetts: Harvard University Press, 2002.
The Holy Bible, New International Version. Grand Rapids, Michigan: Zondervan Publishing House, 1984.

Twelve Southerners. *I'll Take My Stand: The South and the Agrarian Tradition.* c.1930; Baton Rouge: Louisiana State University Press, 1977.

West, M.L. *Hesiod's Works and Days.* Oxford: Clarendon Press, 1978.--- *Hesiod, Theogony, Works and Days.* Oxford: Oxford University Press, 1988.

Whybray R.N.. *Wealth and Poverty in the Book of Proverbs.* Sheffield, England: Sheffield Academic Press, 1990. --- *The Book Of Proverbs.* Cambridge University Press, 1972.

Wirzba, Norman (ed.). *The Art of the Commonplace: the Agrarian Essays of Wendell Berry.* Washington D.C.: Shoemaker and Hoard, 2003.

SELECT BIBLIOGRAPHY I: AGRARIANISM

Agar, Herbert & Tate, Allen. *Who Owns America? A New Declaration of Independence* 1936; Wilmington, Delaware: ISI Books, 1999.
Angal, Andrew J. *Wendell Berry.* Twayne Publishers, 1995.
Aston, T.H. & C.H.E Philpin (eds.), *The Brenner Debate: Agrarian Class Structure and economic development in pre-industrial Europe.* Cambridge, 1985.
Barrel, Pierre. *Les Agrariens français de Méline à Pisani.* Paris : A. Colin, 1968.
Beer, M. *An Inquiry into Physiocracy.* London: Allen & Unwin, 1939.
Berry, Wendell. *Citizenship Papers.* Emeryville, Ca.: Shoemaker & Hoard, 2004.
-----. *The Gift of Good Land.* San Francisco: North Point Press, 1982.
-----. *The Unsettling of America: Culture and Agriculture.* New York: Harcourt Brace Jovanovich, 1977.
-----. *A Place on Earth.* New York: Harcourt, Brace, and World, 1967.
-----. *The Way of Ignorance.* Emeryville, Ca.: Shoemaker & Hoard, 2006.
Bingham, Emily S. & Underwood, Thomas A. *The Southern Agrarians and the New Deal: Essays After I'll Take My Stand.* University of Virginia Press, 2001.
Campbell, Mildred. *The English Yeoman Under Elizabeth and the Early Stuarts.* New York: Augustus Kelly, 1968.
Carlson, Allan. *The New Agrarian Mind; the Movement toward Decentralist Thought in Twentieth-Century America.* New Brunswick, N.J.: Transaction, 2000.
Chinard, Gilbert. Jefferson and the Physiocrats. In *The Correspondence of Thomas Jefferson and Pierre Samuel du Pont de Nemours, 1798 1817.* Edited by Dumas Malone, translated by Linwood Lehman. New York: Da Capo, 1970.
Conkin, Paul. *The Southern Agrarians.* Knoxville: University of Tennessee Press, 1988.
Cowan, Louise. *The Fugitive Group: A Literary History.* Baton Rouge: Louisiana State University Press, 1959.
Edwards, Everett E. *Jefferson and Agriculture: A Sourcebook.* Published by US Department of Agriculture, 1943.
Ellis, F. *Peasant Economics. Farm Households and Agrarian Development.* Cambridge: Cambridge University Press, 2003.
Freyfogle, Eric T. *Agrarianism and the Good Society: Land, Culture, Conflict, and Hope.* University of Kentucky Press, 2007.

---------. *Why Conservation is Failing and how It Gan Gain Ground.* New Haven: Yale University Press, 2006.
---------. *The Land we Share: Private Property and the Common Good.* Washington D.C.: Island Press, 2003.
---------. *The New Agrarianism: Land, Culture, and the Community of Life.* Washington D.C.: Island Press, 2001.
Griswold, A. Whitney. *Farming and Democracy.* New Haven: Yale University Press, 1952.
Heitland, W.E. *Agricola.* Cambridge: Cambridge University Press, 1921.
Howard, Sir Albert & Berry, Wendell. *The Soil and Health: A Study of Organic Agriculture.* University of Kentucky Press, 2006.
Jackson, Wes. *New Roots for Agriculture.* San Francisco: Friends of the Earth, 1980.
Jegen, Mary Evelyn, and Brunno Manno (eds.). *The Earth Is the Lord's: Essays on Stewardship.* New York: Paulist Press, 1978.
Johnson, Arthur H. *The Disappearance of the Small Landowner.* 1909; Oxford: Oxford University Press, 1963.
Landry, Donna. *The Invention of the Countryside: Hunting, Walking, and Ecology in English Literature, 1671-1831.* Palgrave Macmillan, 2001.
Leverette, William E., Jr. and David E. Shi. "Herbert Agar and *Free America*: A Jeffersonian Alternative to the New Deal." *Journal of American Studies* 16 (Aug.1982): 189-206.
Livi-Bacci, M. *A Concise History of World Population.* 4th ed.. Malden, MA: Blackwell Pub. 2007.
Logsdon, Gene. *The Mother of All Arts: Agrarianism and the Creative Impulse.* University of Kentucky Press, 2007.
Magagna, V. 1991. *Communities of Grain. Rural Rebellion in Comparative Perspective.* Ithaca & London: Cornell University Press, 1991.
Marx, Leo. *The Machine in the Garden: Technology and the Pastoral Ideal in America.* 1964; Oxford: Oxford University Press, 1999.
Mclain, James J. *The Economic Writings of Du Pont de Nemours.* Newark: University of Delaware Press, c.1977.
McRae, Andrew. *God Speed the Plough: the Representation of Agrarian England, 1500-1660.* Cambridge: Cambridge University Press, 2004.
Ochiai, Akiko. *Harvesting Freedom: African American Agrarianism in Civil War Era South Carolina.* Praeger Publishers, 2004.
Prothero, R.E. (Lord Ernle). *English Farming: Past and Present.* Chap.3-7. Chicago: Quadrangle Books, 1961.
Sallares, R. *Ecology of the Ancient Greek World.* Ithaca, N.Y.: 1991.

Schusky, E.L. *Culture and Agriculture. An Ecological Introduction to Traditional and Modern Farming Systems.* New York: Bergin & Garvey, 1989.

Shapiro, Edward S. "Catholic Agrarian Thought and the New Deal." *Catholic Historical Review* 65 (Oct.1979): 583-99.

Slovic, Scott. *Seeking Awareness in American Nature Writing: Henry David Thoreau, Annie Dillard, Edward Abbey, Wendell Berry, Barry Lopez.* Salt Lake City, Utah: University of Utah Press, 1992.

Summerhill, Thomas. *Harvest of Dissent: Agrarianism in Central New York in the Nineteenth Century.* University of Illinois Press, 2005.

Tawney, R.H. *The Agrarian Problem in the Sixteenth Century.* Reprint of the 1912 ed. New York: Harper Torchbooks, 1967.

Teres, Harvey M. "Toward a Healthy Community: An Interview with Wendell Berry." *Christian Century,* 15 (Oc.1997) 912.

Thirsk, Joan. *The Agrarian History of England and Wales.* Cambridge: Cambridge University Press, 1967.

Thomas, M. *Agrarianism in American Literature.* Bobbs-Merrill Co., 1969.

Toutain, Jules. *The Economic Life of the Ancient World.* Translated by M.R. Dobie. New York: A.A. Knopf, 1930.

Vaggi, Gianni. *The Economics of François Quesnay.* Durham: Duke University Press, 1987.

Weber, Max. *The Agrarian Sociology of Ancient Civilizations.* Trans. by R.I. Frank. London, MLB, 1909; repr. Atlantic Highlands, N.J.: Humanities Press, 1976.

Wirzba, Norman & Kingsolver, Barbara. *The Essential Agrarian Reader.* Washington D.C.: Shoemaker and Hoard, 2004.

Wood, J.W. "A theory of Preindustrial Population Dynamics. Demography, Economy, and Well-Being in Malthusian Systems. *Current Anthropology* 39:99-135.

Wood, Neal. *John Locke and Agrarian Capitalism.* Berkeley: University of California Press, 1984.

------. "Decentralist Intellectuals and the New Deal. *Journal of American History* 58 (Mar.1972) 938-57.

SELECT BIBLIOGRAPHY II: HESIOD

Amouretti, Marie-Claire. *Le Pain et l'huile dans la Grèce antique.* Paris : Annales Littéraires de l'Université de Besançon, 1986.

---------. « Les céréals dans l'antiquité : Éspèces, mouture et conservation, liaison et interférence dans la Grèce classique, » in M. Gast and F. Sigaut (eds.), *Les techniques de conservation des graines à long terme* (Paris 1979), 57-69.

Amyard, A. "L'idée du travail et autarche individuelle, "*Revue d'histoire de la philosophie* in *Études d'histoire ancienne* (Paris 1968), 461-73.

Athanassakis, Apostolos N. "Introduction", in *Ramus* 21 (1992) 1-10.

Bintliff, J.L. "The archaeological survey of the valley of the Muses and its significance for Boeotian history." In *La Montagne des Muses,* ed. by A. Hurst & A. Schachter, 193-224. Genève, 1996.

--------, & Kostas Sbonias (eds.). *Reconstructing Past Population Trends in Mediterranean Europe (3000 BC-AD 1800).* Oxford: Oxbow Books, 1999.

Braun, T. "Barley Cakes and Emmer Bread." In *Food in Antiquity,* ed. by J. Wilkins, D. Harvey, and M. Dobson, 25-37. Exeter, 1995.

Buck, R.J. *The History of Boeotia.* University of Alberta Press: Edmonton, 1979.

Burford, Alison. *Land and Labor in the Greek World.* Baltimore: John Hopkins University Press, 1993.

Claus, David. B. "Defining Moral Terms in the Works and Days." Transactions of the American Philological Association 107 (1977): 73 84.

Dalton, George, ed. *Tribal and Peasant Economies: Readings in Economic Anthropology.* Garden City, N.Y.: National History Press, Doubleday, 1967.

Detienne, Marcel. "Crise agraire et attitude religieuse chez Hésiode. " Collection Latomus, *Revue des Études Latines,* no.68. Brussels: Berchem, 1963.

Edwards, A. "Homer's Ethical Geography: Country and City in the *Odyssey.*" *Transactions of the American Philological Association* 123: 27-78.

Finley, M.I. *World of Odysseus.* 2nd ed. Middlesex, 1979.

Fisher, N. & H. van Wees. *Archaic Greece: New Approaches and New Evidence.* London, 1998.

Fossey, J.M. *Togography and Population of Ancient Boeotia.* Vol.1. Chicago, 1988.

--------. *Papers in Boeotian Topography and History.* Amsterdam, 1990.
--------. *Boeotia Antiqua II. Papers on Recent Work in Boeotian Archaeology and Epigraphy.* Amsterdam, 1992.
Gallant, Thomas W. *Risk and Survival in Ancient Greece: Reconstructing the Rural Domestic Economy.* Stanford: Stanford University Press, 1991.
Garnsey, P. *Famine and Food Supply in the Graeco-Roman World. Responses to Risk and Crisis.* Cambridge, 1988.
Gauvin, G., & J. Morin. "Le site d'Ascra et ses carriers." In *Boeotia Antiqua II. Papers*
Halstead, P & G. Jones. "Agrarian Ecology in the Greek Islands: Time, Stress, Scale, and Risk." *Journal of Hellenic Studies* 109 (1989): 41 55.
Isager, S & Skydsgaard. *Ancient Greek Agriculture.* London & New York, 1992.
Kaneloupolos, Charles. "L'Agriculture d'Hésiode: Techniques et culture." *Éditions de la Maison des Sciences de l'Homme* 15 (1990) : 131-158.
Marsilio, M. *Farming and Poetry in Hesiod's Works and Days.* Landam, Md.: University Press of America, 2000.
Mezzadri, Bernard. "La Double Éris initiale." *Métis* 4 (1989): 51-60.
Mitchell, G. & P.J. Rhodes (eds.). *The Development of the Polis in Archaic Greece.* London: Routledge, 1997.
Murray, O. & Price S.. *The Greek City from Homer to Alexander.* Oxford: Oxford University Press, 1990.
Nilsson, Martin P. *Greek Folk Religion.* Philadelphia, PA: University of Pennsylvania Press, 1998.
Osborne, R. *Classical Landscape with Figures: the Ancient Greek City and its Countryside.* Dobbs Ferry, NY: Sheridan House,1987.
Rackham, O. "Observations on the Historical Ecology of Boeotia." *Annual of the British School at Athens* 78: 291-351.
Rich, J.& A. Wallace-Hadrill. *City and Country in the Ancient World.* London & New York: Routledge, 1991.
Richardson, N.J. and S. Piggott. "Hesiod's Waggon: Text and Technology." Journal of Hellenic Studies 102 (1982): 225-29.
Roberts, W. Rhys. *The Ancient Boeotians: Their Character and Culture, and their Reputation.* Cambridge: Cambridge University Press, 1895.
Snodgrass, A.M. "The site of Ascra." In *Béotie Antique,* ed. by P. Roesch and G. Argoud, 87-95. Actes du Colloque International "La Béotie Antique" à Lyons et à Saint Étienne du 16 mai au 20 mai 1983. Paris, 1985.
---------. *The Dark Age of Greece.* 1971; Routledge, 2000.

----------. *Archaic Greece: The Age Of Experiment*. Berkeley: University of California Press, 1981.
Tandy, D. *Warriors into Traders: the Power of the Market in Early Greece.* Berkeley: University of California Press, 1997.
Thalmann, W.G. *The Swineherd and the Bow. Representations of Class in the Odyssey.* Ithaca & London: Cornell University Press, 1998.
Thomas, C.G. & C. Conant. *From Citadel to City-State: the Transformation of Greece, 1200-700 B.C.E.* Bloomington: Indiana University Press,1999.
Walcot, Peter. *Greek Peasants, Ancient and Modern.* Manchester: Manchester University Press, 1991.
Wallace, Paul. "Hesiod and the Valley of the Muses." *Greek, Roman, and Byzantine Studies* 15:1 (1974):4-24.
Welles, C. Bradford. "Hesiod's Attitude toward Labor." *Greek, Roman, and Byzantine Studies* 8 (1967): 5-23.
Wender, Dorothea S. *Hesiod and Theognis.* New York: Penguin, 1973.
Whitley, J., *Style and Society in Dark Age Greece: The Changing Face of a Pre-literate Society, 1100-700 BC* (Cambridge, 2003).
Wilamowitz-Moellendorff, U. von. *Hesiodos Erga.* Berlin, ed.1962.

SELECT BIBLIOGRAPHY III: PROVERBS

Aharoni, Y. *The Land of the Bible: a Historical Geography.* Trans. by A.F. Rainey; Philadelphia: Westminster Press, c.1979

Blidstein, Gerald. "Man and Nature in the Sabbatical Year." *Tradition: A Journal of Orthodox Thought* 8, no.4 (1966): 48-55. Reprinted in *Judaism andEnvironmental Ethics: A Reader,* edited by Martin D. Yaffe, 136-42 (Landam, Md.: Lexington Books, 2001).

Borowski, O. *Agriculture in Iron Age Israel.* American School of Oriental Research, 2002.

Carmell, Aryeh. "Judaism and the Quality of the Environment." In *Challenge: Torah Views on Science and Its Problems,* edited by Aryeh Carmell & Cyril Domb, 500-525. New York: Ktav, 1983.

Cohen, Jeremy, *"Be Fertile and Increase, Fill the Earth and Master It": The Ancient and Medieval Career of a Biblical Text.* Ithaca, New York: Cornell University Press, 1989.

Coote, Robert B. *Early Israel: A New Horizon.* Minneapolis: Fortress Press, 1990.

Ehrenfeld, David, and Phillip J. Bentley. "Judaism and the Practice of Stewardship. *Judaism and Environmental Ethics: A Reader,* edited by Martin D. Yaffe, 125-35 (Landam, Md.: Lexington Books, 2001).

Eisenberg, Evan. *The Ecology of Eden.* New York: Alfred A. Knopf, 1998.

Gordis, Robert. "Job and Ecology (and the Significance of Job 40:15)." *Hebrew Annual Review* 9 (1985): 189-202.

Hareuveni, Nogah. *Nature and our Biblical Heritage.* Kiryat Ono, Israel: Neot Kedumin, 1980.

Hiebert, Theodore. *The Yahwist's Landscape: Nature and Religion in Early Israel* Oxford: Oxford University Press, 1996.

Hillel, D. *Out of the Earth: Civilization and the Life of the Soil.* New York: Free Press, c.1991.

Hopkins, David C. *The Highlands of Canaan: Agricultural Life in the Early Iron Age* Sheffield, England: Almond, 1985.

Kay, Jeanne. "Comments on the Unnatural Jew." *Environmental Ethics* 7 (1985): 189 191: *Judaism and Environmental Ethics: A Reader,* edited by Martin D. Yaffe, 86-104 (Landam, Md.: Lexington Books, 2001).

Kugel, James A. *The Idea of Biblical Poetry: Parallelism and its History.* New Haven: Yale University Press, 1981.

Murphy, Roland Edmund. *The Tree of Life: An Exploration of Biblical Wisdom Literature.* 3rd ed. Wm. B. Eedrmans Publishing Company, 2002.
Novak, David. "Technology and Its Ultimate Threat: A Jewish Meditation." *Research in Philosophy and Technology* 10 (1990): 43-70.
Packer, J.I. & Soderlund, Sven K (eds.). *The Way of Wisdom.* Zondervan, 2000.
Reifenberg, A. *The Struggle between the Desert and the Sown: Rise and Fall of Agriculture in the Levant.* With an intro. By W.C. Lowdermilk; Jerusalem: Publishing Department of the Jewish Agency, 1955.
Tamari, Meir. *With All Your Possessions: Jewish Ethics and Economic Life.* New York: Free Press; and London: Collier Macmillan, 1987.
Toperov, Shlomo Pesach. *The Animal Kingdom in Jewish Thought.* Northvale N.J.: Jason Aronson, 1995.
Yaffe, Martin D. *Judaism and Environmental Ethics: A Reader* (Landam, Md.: Lexington Books, 2001).

NOTES

[1] For more on the organization of Mycenaean land-ownership see: P Halstead, *Proceedings of the Cambridge Philological Society,* 1992, 57ff.
[2] Robyn Osborne; in: Anthony T. Edwards, *Hesiod's Ascra.* (University of California Press, 2004) 26-27.
[3] Carol Thomas and Craig Conant (1999, xviii-xxi); in: Edwards, 26-27.
[4] Victor Davis Hanson, *The Other Greek: the Family Farm and the Agrarian Roots of Western Civilization.* (The Free Press, 1995) 28.
[5] Hanson, 32.
[6] Ibid.,43.
[7] Ibid., 37.
[8] Charles Freeman, *Egypt, Greece, and Rome: Civilizations of the Ancient Mediterranean.* (Oxford, 1996) 85.
[9] For information on further scholarship regarding the context portrayed in Homer see: Morris, I. "The Use and Abuse of Homer". *Classical Antiquity* 5 (1986), 81-138; Whitley, J., *Style and Society in Dark Age Greece: The Changing Face of a Pre-literate Society, 1100-700 BC* (Cambridge, 2003).
[10] Hanson, 7.
[11] Here is a list of other references to agriculture in Homer: (Il. 14.122-124); (Od. 7.113, 11.489-91, 18.24, 18.357-76. There is a noticeable derth of ecocriticism on the Homeric epics. The following will hopefully provide an entry into the field: J. O' Sullivan. "Nature and Culture in Odyssey 9." *Symbolae Osloenses* 65.7-17 (1990); J. Redfield, *Nature and Culture in the Iliad* (Chicago, 1975); S. Shein, "Odysseus and Polyphemus in the Odyssey", *Greek, Roman, and Byzantine Studies* 11.73-83.
[12] David W. Tandy & Walter C. Neale, *Hesiod's Works and Days.* (University of California Press, 1996) 30. They state that five to ten acres of it was in "vegetables", as well as some olive and fruit and trees; the authors do not specify whether "vegetables" includes grains, but that much of a farmer's land used to grow vegetables, as in a garden, sounds high.
[13] V.N. Andreyev, "Some Aspects of Agrarian Conditions in Attica in the Fifth to Third Century," *Eirene* 12 (1974), 14-15. (In Hanson, 188).
[14] Hanson, 188.
[15] M.I. Finley, *Economy and Society in Ancient Greece* (London, 1981) 65. (In Hanson, 188).
[16] Hanson, 186. Although the figures referenced in notes 19-21 come from Attica during the better documented fifth century, Hanson argues for continuity and

semblance between city-states in this respect (Hanson, 21), and so these can hopefully give us a ballpark estimate of conditions for Hesiod's time.

[17] Bintliff and Snodgrass (1985, 140-143). In Edwards, 17.

[18] Hugh G. Evelyn-White. *Hesiod: Homeric Hymns, Epic Cycle, Homerica.* (1914; Cambridge, Mass. & London: Loeb, 1998). All quotes in English and Greek are from this edition unless otherwise stated.

[19] There is scholarly contention as to whether Hesiod authored the third section of the poem. See: Hermann Fränkel, *Early Greek Poetry and Philosophy.* (New York & London: Harcourt Brace Jovanovich, 1973) 129.

[20] West calls this praise of a miserable meal "a conscious paradox": essentially, "better something than nothing". ML West. *Hesiod's Works and Days.* (Greek text with notes) (Oxford, Clarendon Press, 1978) 153.

[21] Fränkel agreed with this definition of wealth in Hesiod. He writes, "'Wealth' probably signifies no more than having enough to eat once a day the year through...". Fränkel, 124.

[22]
θῆκε θεῶν κῆρυξ, ὀνόμηνε δὲ τήωδε γυναῖκα/ Πανδώρην, ὅτι πάντεσ 'Ο λυμπια
δώματ' ἔκοντεσ/ δῶρον ἐδώρησαν, πῆμ' ἀνδράσιν ἀλφιηστῆσιν (80-82).

[23] Herodotus is more balanced in describing non-agricultural people and does not always portray them in a negative light (Herodotus IV.19).

[24] Robin Osborne. *Greece in the Making.* (London & New York: Routledge, 1996) 154-155.

[25] οἵ 'ρα θεοῖσι πεποιθότεσ ἀθανάτοισιν/ οὔτε φυτεύουσιν χερσὶν φυτὸν ο ὔτε ἀρόωσι· (115-116).
From French/Greek text: *L'Odyssée « Poésie Homérique » Tome II : Chants VIII-XV.* Texte établi et traduit par Victor Bérard. Neuvième tirage. Paris Société D'Édition « Les Belles Lettres ». 1974.

[26] Nelson, Stephanie A. *God and the Land: the Metaphysics of Farming in Hesiod and Virgil.* Oxford & New York: Oxford University Press, 1998) 37.

[27] In these instances the word is either δμωή or δμώσ.

[28] Εὖτ' ἄν δὲ πρώτιστ' ἄροτοσ θνητοῖσι φανείη,/ δὴ τότ' ἐφορμηθῆναι ὁ μῶσ δμῶέσ τε καὶ αὐτὸσ/ αὔην καὶ διερὴν ἀρότοιο καθ' ὥρην,/ πρωὶ μ άλα σπεύδων, ἵνα τοι πλήθωσιν ἄρουραι. (458-462)

[29] M.L West, *Hesiod, Theogony, Works and Days,* (Oxford University Press, 1988).

[30] James A. Montmarquet, *The Idea of Agrarianism.* (Moscow, Idaho: University of Idaho Press, 1989) 32.

[31] For the important distinction between the planter and yeoman classes in the antebellum South, see Andrew Nelson Lytle's essay "The Hind Tit" in *I'll Take*

My Stand, and for a discussion of the Southern yeoman class specifically see Frank Lawrence Owsley's *Plain Folk of the Old South* (1949).

[32] It is difficult to say if this has changed recently in a significant way, although the increased legitimacy of the environmental movement may have effects in this area if small-farming continues to grow in its association with it. And yet this is still one step removed from legal protection or political advocacy in the public forum, and actual perpetuation.

[33] Thomas Jefferson was obviously a distinguished advocate of these ideas. For his views on this subject see: Everett E. Edwards. *Jefferson and Agriculture: A Sourcebook*. (Published by US Department of Agriculture, 1943); also: Whitney A. Griswold. *Farming and Democracy*. (New Haven: Yale University Press, 1952).

[34] Tandy and Neale, 68 (nt.43).

[35] In a word, Hesiod's view of women is "pessimistic." In the poem he continues along the track that he set out in the *Theogony*, which casts Pandora as the unambiguous ruin of all and sundry. This study is not aware of monographs on women in agrarianism per se, although the following might offer an introduction to the more general subject: P. Herfst, *Le Travail de la femme dans la Grèce ancienne* (1922); D.M. Schaps, *Economic Rights of Women in Ancient Greece* (1979); J. Archer et al (eds.), *Women in Ancient Societies* (1994).

[36] Of the translations available, that in French with the Greek text facing by Paul Mazon (1947) was very good; the Greek/English translations in English are not as convincing or fluid; of the English only Hines's new translation passes as quite good (2005), as well as Tandy and Neale's (1996).

[37] A standardized text of Hesiod did not appear until Rzach's *Hesiodi Carmina* (1902). (Tandy and Neale, 2).

[38] Wilamowitz-Moellendorff, U. von. *Hesiodos Erga*. Berlin, ed.1962.

[39] Tandy & Neale, 2.

[40] There is no English translation of Wilamowitz, although there are English editions of Jaeger. Jaeger for his part cites Wilamowitz often, showing that he was the authority up to that point.

[41] Werner Jaeger. *Paideia: the Ideals of Greek Culture*. Vol.1. Trans. by Gilbert Highet. (New York: Oxford University Press, 1945) 58-59.

[42] Jaeger, 62.

[43] Herodotus asserted that both Homer and Hesiod had lived 400 years before his own time, that is, about 830-820 BC. Hugh G. Evelyn-White. *Hesiod: Homeric Hymns, Epic Cycle, Homerica.* (1914; Cambridge, Mass. & London: Loeb, 1998) xxvi. Although the dating of the poem gets into to what degree one sees it as representing Dark Age or polis context. See the discussion for this further on in this section.

[44] Jaeger, 74.

[45] Fränkel, ix.

[46] Ibid., x.
[47] Ibid., 124.
[48] νήπιε Πέρση,/ ἔργα, τά τ' ἀνθρώποισι θεοὶ διετεκμήραντο, (397-398)
[49] Fränkel, 126.
[50] Ibid., 124.
[51] James A. Montmarquet. *The Idea of Agrarianism.* (Moscow, Idaho: University of Idaho Press, 1989). Montmaquet's study has some flaws in the sloppiness of the language and un-factual comments, but it is still an impressive work because of its scope, and as was mentioned is the only one of its kind.
[52] See the work of M.C. Amouretti for example (in Bibliography II).
[53] Lattimore (1959), Wender (1973), Athanassakis (1983), Frazier (1983), West (1988), and Lombardo (1993). In Tandy and Neale, 2-3.
[54] Jeremy Cohen. *"Be Fertile and Increase, Fill the Earth and Master It": The Ancient and Medieval Career of a Biblical oText.* (Ithaca: Cornell University Press, 1989) 268.
[55] See essay "A Secular Pilgrimage" in: Wendell Berry. *A Continuous Harmony* (Washington D.C.: Shoemaker and Hoard, reprint of 1970, 1972 ed.).
[56] I agree with this although I grapple with the extent to which it was a product of the Industrial revolution or was a process that had been going on for a long time and culminated during that period or even later (see Chapter 7).
[57] For another detailing of scholarship on Hesiod see the essay "Introduction" by Apostolos N. Athanassakis, in *Ramus* 21 (1992) 1-10.
[58] The consensus was founded on Edourd Will's 1957 article "Aux Origines Du Régime Foncier Grec, Homère, Hésiode, et L'arrière-Plan Mycénien." *Revue des Études Anciennes* 59 : 5-50. (In Edwards, 1).
[59] Hanson, 125. The main features of Solon's economic legislation appears to be the release of debtor-slaves and the removal of unlawful enclosures, Hanson's characterization speaks to the latter. In general we should keep in mind that the two conspicuous examples of agrarian reforms in antiquity are those of Solon in Attica and the Gracchi in Italy. This study also notes those of Lycurgus in Lacedemonia that Plutarch describes in his life.
[60] Edwards, 4.
[61] Boeotia was dominated by the city of Thebes from circa the 7th century BC; but a number of cities also existed in the territory.
[62] Ibid., xii.
[63] Ibid., 22.
[64] Ibid., 2. The view we have from Theognis is from the other side: the feeling of the aristocracy of being under siege from other classes (Freeman, 182).
[65] For a Marxist reading of *Works and Days*, see: Karl Polanyi. 1977. *The Livelihood of Man.* Academic Press. (ed. By Harry W. Pearson); and for a more recent Marxist overview of major Greek works see: Peter W. Rose, *Sons of the*

Gods, Children of Earth: Ideology and Literary Form in Ancient Greece (Ithaca: Cornell University Press, 1992).
[66] Hanson, 417.
[67] Hanson, 4.
[68] Tandy and Neale, 3.
[69] Ibid., 3.
[70] Ian Morris. *Archeology as Cultural History. Words and Things in Iron Age Greece* (Oxford, 2000) 164, 166.
[71] Edwards, 26.
[72] Hanson, 45. See Appendix C for a more detailed look at γεωργόσ and other Greek terms.
[73] Tandy and Neale, 1.
[74] N. Nelson, *Medieval Agrarian Economy* (New York: Henry Holt & Company, 1936) 7. Nelson says, "The individual farmer with his own land to be cultivated at this own will and in his own way appears rarely, if at all."
[75] David Stockton. *The Classical Athenian Democracy*. (New York, Oxford, Oxford University Press, 1990) 8.
[76] πεντᾱκοσιομεδιμοι (Thuc.3.16) (Arist. Pol. 2.12,6) (Plut. Solon 18); ἱππεῖσ (Thuc. 7.75) for one to be a member of this class one had to possess land producing 300 medimni, a charger, and a hackney for their groom or esquire (Liddell & Scott); ζευγίται, so called for being able to keep a team (ζεῦγοσ) of oxen (Arist. Pol 2.12.6); θῆτεσ (Arist. Pol. 2.12,6; 4.4,10; 6.7,1).
[77] Stockton (1990), 26.
[78] γεωργόσ is the Greek term for "small land-owners" (Arist. Pol. 4.12,3). It is interesting to note that the word does not occur in *Works and Days*. This may mean that it simply never came up or could reinforce the overall picture that Hesiod is not a self-conscious, self-styled farmer who thinks he is anything special, or that farming is a blissful occupation.
[79] Evan Eisenberg, "The Ecology of Eden". In: Hava Tirosh-Samuelson (editor). *Judaism and Ecology: Created World and Revealed Word.* (Cambridge, Massachusetts: Harvard University Press, 2002) 31. This must be referring to some sort of commons.
[80] Ibid, 32.
[81] Ibid, 32.
[82] Although some scholars place this as much as a century later.
[83] "Israel and Judah". The Encyclopaedia of World History. 2001. <http://www.bartleby.com/67/104.html>
[84] "The New Kingdom and the Third Intermediate Period (18th-24th Dynasties)." The Encyclopedia of World History. 2001. <http://www.bartleby.com/67/93.html#c2p00137>
[85] Tirosh-Samuelson, 39.

[86] Hava Tirosh-Samuelson (editor). *Judaism and Ecology: Created World and Revealed Word.* (Cambridge, Massachusetts: Harvard University Press, 2002).
[87] Eisenberg, Evan. *The Ecology of Eden.* New York: Alfred A. Knopf, 1998.
[88] Tirosh-Samuelson, 43. Peake's commentary on the Bible concludes with Eisenberg that the second creation account in Genesis (the Yahwist account) locates Eden in Palestine. From Matthew Black & HH Rowley. *Peake's Commentary on the Bible.* (London & Edinburgh: Thomas Nelson Ltd., 1962) 179-180.
[89] Ibid, 45.
[90] Ibid, 39-41.
[91] Ibid, 34.
[92] Ibid, 39. He does not give evidence to clarify the exact nature of the Egyptian influence or involvement. Another interesting point Eisenberg raises is that Ezek. 28.12-16, which refers of the king Tyre as having been in Eden, describes the history of the Canaanites. This would trace the descendents of the Canaanites through Tyre to the Carthaginians. This is not usually thought of when Carthage is being discussed.
[93] This intimate knowledge of local geography found in Joshua is noteworthy because it argues both that the book was written after the Israelites had lived in the Promised Land for quite some time, and that the Israelites knew and loved every nook and cranny of it.
[94] All quotes from the Bible are the following translation unless otherwise stated: *The Holy Bible, New International Version.* (Grand Rapids, Michigan: Zondervan Publishing House, 1984).
[95] "redemption" or "right or price of redemp." (*geullah*): Lev.27.20, Ruth 4.7; Jer.32.7, 32.8; "to free" (by avenging or repaying) (*gaal*) (in agricultural sense): Lev.25.25, 25.26, 25.48, 25.49; Lev.27.13, 27.15, 27.19, 27.20, 27.31; Ruth 4.4, 4.6; (in non-agricultural sense): Gen.48.16; Ex.6.6; Psalms 69.18, 72.14, 74.2, 77.15, 103.4; Isa.43.1, 44.22, 48.26; Lamentations 3.58; Hos.13.14; Mic.4.10; "freedom" or "redemption" (*geullah*): Lev.25.26, 25.29, 25.32; "to be or become freed" or "redeemed" (gaal)(2): Lev.25.30, 25.54; Lev.27.20, 27.27, 27.28, 27.33. Leviticus chapter 27.16-25 is also a detailing of the contingencies and requirements surrounding "sanctifying" and "redeeming" a field.
[96] *bet av.* Tirosh-Samuelson, 41.
[97] mishpahah. Ibid, 41.
[98] Ibid, 42.
[99] Ibid, 38-39.
[100] Ibid, 39.
[101] Ibid, 27. Eisenberg in the first instance is denoting the Canaanite and Israelite, which I extend to the Archaic Greek, and in the second the Babylonian, Assyrian, and Egyptian. Historian Donald Worster makes the type of irrigation system a

society practices central to his thesis in *Rivers of Empire* (Oxford University Press, 1992).

[102] Isa.5:8; Joel 1:1-12; 2:21-27; Hos.4:1-3 etc. The books of the major and minor prophets hold much for agrarian analysis. The *Catholic Encyclopaedia*, whose entry on agrarianism shows an in depth knowledge of the sources, says in referring to the Prophets that, "the main social problem was the preservation of a free peasantry…" This leaves the door wide open for analysis. "Agrarianism," *Catholic Encyclopedia,* (1907).

[103] There are many ancient and modern examples of this. For example, the Roman "bread and circuses" and the New Deal. For the unquestionably best discussion of this subject to which the author is openly indebted, see De Tocqueville. Alexis De Tocqueville. *De la Démocratie en Amérique I.* (Édition Gallimard, 1961), 148-149, 162-163, especially 318, also 390; *Vol.II* : 422, 424-425, 427, 342, 432-438.

[104] The section on criticism contains more on the subject of dates. The book of Proverbs begins with the statement that these are the proverbs of Solomon son of David, king of Israel (Prov. 1.1).

[105] In fact the Old Testament seems to represent each of these classes in its different books: the Torah being the proof the existence of the priests, the major and minor prophetic books of the prophets, and the wisdom literature of the counsel of the elders (this last also known as the "counsel of the wise").

[106] A. Cohen. *Proverbs.* (1946; London, Jerusalem, New York: The Soncino Press, 1985) xi.

[107] A. Cohen, xi.

[108] Ibid., xi.

[109] See Psalm 137.

[110] For the period leading up to the first exile, there is also the evidence of the strange carrot dangled in front of the noses of the besieged residents of Jerusalem by the Assyrians during the reign of Hezekiah (c.715-686 BC), where the Assyrian commander enjoins them to, "Make peace with me and come out to me. Then every one of you will eat from his own vine and fig tree and drink water from his own cistern, until I come and take you to a land like your own, a land of grain and wine, a land of bread and vineyards, a land of olive trees and honey…" The Assyrian social structure was one employing mass slave-gangs of Arameans who eventually took over the former empire of their masters—not one of small independent farmers. So the Assyrian's taunts could be a reference to a system or practice for which the Jews were known.

[111] The Hebrew word for proverb is *mishlë,* found in several contexts outside of Proverbs. In Job 13.12, and Ecclesiastes 12.9. it means something along the lines of our "maxim" or "proverb", but in Job 27.1 and 29.1 it means something like "discourse."

[112] Other translations of the Bible divide the book of Proverbs at different points.

[113] Or "Even a fool is thought wise if he keeps silent, and discerning if he holds his tongue (17.28)."
[114] Or "Better to meet a bear robs of her cubs than a fool in his folly (17.12)."
[115] If a simple "right and wrong" dualism were the case here, the following proverbs (to cite a few examples) would not fit: "Many are the plans of a man's heart, but it is the Lord's purpose that prevails (19.21)" or "A kin's rage is like the roar of a lion, but his favor is like dew on the grass (19.12)". To state it another way, the parallel structure does not evidence a belief in some abstract "right and wrong" than one can impose upon every situation, but rather a belief that truth is arrived at through the experience of real-life situations, and is best illustrated through two situations or ideas that clarify each other. This demonstrates a practical mindset, and is the derivative of the agricultural society from which the proverbs originated. For a respected work of scholarship on the parallelism of Hebrew proverbs, see: James L. Kugel. *The Idea of Biblical Poetry: Parallelism and its History.* (New Haven: Yale University Press, 1981).
[116] The section on criticism, c), will relate the views of scholars regarding such questions of origin.
[117] R.N. Whybray, *Wealth and Poverty in the Book of Proverbs* (Sheffield, England: Sheffield Academic Press) 9. It is assumed that Whybray is referring to the social group among whom the proverbs originated.
[118] Whybray (1990), 62.
[119] The author confesses genuine regret that he is not able to read one of the two languages (Hebrew) of the works he has chosen to compare. He is usually the first to consider knowledge of original languages to be essential to an accurate reading of a work. However, the lack of ecocritical analysis of Proverbs, and the implications of the comparative study hopefully excuse the lack of qualification for the undertaking.
[120] A. Cohen, xiv.
[121] R.N. Whybray, *The Book Of Proverbs* (Cambridge University Press, 1972) 16.
[122] However, this study must be careful not to draw a neat division between the Law and the Hebrew wisdom literature, as one scholar (Peter Enns) has rightly pointed out that the Wisdom literature of the Old Testament is in many ways interpreting the Law. The awareness of this point came by word of mouth.
[123] Whybray (1972), xiv.
[124] For example, we don't think it sounds strange for an English proverbs to say, "Enough is as good as a feast" and not "Enough is as good as a feast for an Englishman".
[125] Agriculture: 10.5, 11.26, 12.11, 13.23, 20.4, 23.10, 24.30-34, 27.18, 27.22, 27.23-27, 28.19(*), 31.16. Because many of the proverbs are self-contained units (not related to the next), while a minority span more than one, "passage" will be used instead of "verse" to cover both instances.
[126] Work and hunger: : 10.3, 12.9, 12.11, 20.13, 28.21(*).

[127] Work: 10.4, 12.24, 12.27, 13.4, 14.23, 18.9, 19, 24, 21.25, 26.15.
[128] Neighbors: 3.28-29, 6.1-5, 11.9, 11.12, 13.25, 14.21, 15.17, 21.10, 24.28, 25.17, 25.18, 26.18-19, 27.10, 27.14, and 29.5.
[129] Wealth and poverty: 6.10-11, 10.2, 10.15, 10.22, 11.4, 11.24, 11.28, 13.11, 13.18, 14.20, 14.24, 15.6, 15.16, 16.8, 18.11, 20.21, 21.5, 21.6, 21.17, 22.16.
[130] Whybray (1990), 13.
[131] Ibid, 23.
[132] A. Cohen, 56.
[133] For the injunctions in the Torah referring to firstfruits see Deuteronomy 18.4, and 26.1-15.
[134] The information concerning this point came by word of mouth.
[135] Whybray (1972), 172.
[136] Ibid, 172. Whybray says here that Agur's sayings probably originally did not extend past the first three, possibly four verses.
[137] According to the Law, such vulnerable cases were under the special protection of Yahweh (Exodus 22.22-24, Deuteronomy 10.18-19). Proverbs 15.25 however does refer to a widow owning land
[138] Whybray (1990), 38.
[139] See 5.1-14, & 6.20-7.27.
[140] Leviticus 20.10
[141] See Proverbs 1.20, 3.13-18, 4.6, 8.1, 9.1-12, and 14.33. Greek culture also personifies wisdom as a woman, although apparently Hesiod saw otherwise in this respect.
[142] However, apparently these two nouns in the Hebrew are cognates, which means that the verse may be referring to two types of the same thing, either vineyards or fields. Although the NIV and the KJV make the distinction.
[143] Tirosh-Samuelson, 56-57.
[144] Eisenberg goes on: "For a clear presentation of this general approach, see Robert B. Coote, *Early Israel: A New Horizon* (Minneapolis: Fortress Press, 1990)...On the ecology and husbandry of ancient Israel, see Aharoni, *The Land of the Bible;* David C. Hopkins, *The Highlands of Canaan: Agricultural Life in the Early Iron Age* (Sheffield, England: Almond, 1985); Borowski, *Agriculture in Iron Age Israel;* Reifenberg, *The Struggle between the Desert and the Sown;* Hillel, *Out of the Earth;* and the eccentric but interesting works of Nogah Hareuveni, founder of the biblical landscape garden Ne'ot Kedumin." (Tirosh-Samuelson, 56-57). He also notes that Theodore Hiebert, a Harvard scholar, shares many of his views on nature in ancient Israel in his *The Yahwist's Landscape: Nature and Religion in Early Israel* (Oxford: Oxford University Press, 1996). (Ibid., 57)
[145] Whybray (1990), 44 (nt.1). He lists as expressing this view: A. Kuschke, "Arm und reich im Alten Testament mit besonderer Berücksichtigung der nachexilischen Zeit", ZAW 57 (1939), p.47; R. Gordis, "The Social Background of Wisdom

Literature", HUCA 18 (1943/44), p.77-118; H.J. Hermisson, *Studien zur israeliteschen Spruchweisheit* (1968), p.94-96; B.V. Malchow, "Social Justice in the Wisdom Literature" (1982); Coggins, "The Old Testament and the Poor" ET 99 (1987-88), p.11-14; T.R. Hobbs, "Reflections on 'the Poor' and the Old Testament", ET 100 (1988-89), p.291-294.

[146] For Near Eastern sources that may have influenced or are comparable to the Wisdom books in the Bible, see: James B. Pritchard. *Ancient Near Eastern Texts Relating to the Old Testament.* (Princeton, 3'rd ed. w/ supplements, 1969). This is the classic source for English language scholarship of scholarly translations of Egyptian, Sumerian, Akkadian, Hittite, Babylonian, and Assyrian documents; from annotated bibliography in: Rev. Joseph W. Gaspar. *Social Ideas in the Wisdom Literature of the Old Testament.* (Washington DC: The Catholic University of America Press, 1947).

[147] Whybray (1990), 59.

[148] M. Lurje. *Studien zur Geschichte der wirtschaftlichen und sozialen Verhältnisse im israelitisch-jüdischen Reich* [1927]. (BZAW 45: Töpelmann, 1927) 17-19. From Whybray (1990), 45 (nt.1).

[149] von Rad made this point, in opposition to Hermisson and Skladny (*Die ältesten Spruchsammlungen in Israel [1962]),* in *Weisheit in Israel* (Neukirchener Verlag, 1970) 105; ET: *Wisdom in Israel.* (London: SCM, 1972) 76. The "magisterial" study Whybray refers to is: G. von Rad. *Theologie des Alten Testament I.* (Munich: Kaiser, 1957). ET: *Old Testament Theology I.* (Edinburgh & London: Olivier & Boyd, 1962

[150] A. Cohen, ix.

[151] Ibid., xi.

[152] Ibid, xiii.

[153] Whybray (1972), 3.

[154] Ibid, 2.

[155] Ibid, 2-3. Whybray cites 25.11-12 as an example.

[156] Ibid, 4.

[157] Ibid, 7.

[158] Ibid, 6.

[159] Whybray (1990), 9.

[160] Ibid, 31.

[161] bid, 31.

[162] Ibid, 36. Leviticus 19.9-12 says, "When you reap the harvest of your land, do not reap to the very edges of you field or gather the gleanings of you harvest. Do not go over your vineyard a second time or pick up the grapes that have fallen. Leave them for the poor and alien. I am the Lord your God. Do not steal. Do not lie. Do not deceive one another. Do not swear falsely by the name of your God. I am the Lord (et al)."

[163] Ibid, 34.

[164] Ibid, 34 , 40.
[165] I Samuel 5.5-9 says, "The king (David) and his men marched to Jerusalem to attack the Jebusites who lived there...David then took up residence in the fortress and called it the City of David. He built up the area around it, from the supporting terraces inward."
[166] "The root *kbš* is a common Semitic root, appearing in most Semitic languages...Its meaning corresponds almost without exception to that of Hebrew. In the OT, there are 14 occurrences in various stems...The meaning can always be rendered by "subdue" it does not vary in the different stems." From: Johannes Botterbueck, Helmer Ringgren, Heinz-Josef Fabry. *Theological Dictionary of the Old Testament*. Vol.VII (Grand Rapids & Cambridge: Wm. B. Eerdmans Publishing Co., 1995) 52. As for the second verb: "*Rdh,* often reinforced by terms of harshness, refers in general to the ruler over slaves, subjects, or enemies, at times to the vanquishing of an opponent in battle, and perhaps even to the trampling upon grapes in a winepress." From: J. Cohen, 16. For an in depth discussion of the exegetical history of this verse see Jeremy Cohen's book, *"Be Fertile and Increase, Fill the Earth and Master It": The Ancient and Medieval Career of a Biblical Text.* See also: J. Cohen, "The Bible, Man, and Nature in the History of Western Thought: A Call for Reassessment." *Journal of Religion* 65 (1985), 155-172; D. Jobling, "'And Have Dominion...': The Interpretation of Old Testament Texts Concerning Man's Rule over the Creation (Genesis 1:26, 28,, 9:1-2, Psalm 8:7-9) from 200 B.C. to the time of the Council of Nicea." Th.D. Dissertation, Union Theological Seminary, New York, 1972. (Cohen says of Jobling's work: "Despite his methodological shortcomings, Jobling's dissertation is a meticulously indexed, invaluable florilegium of Jewish, Gnostic, classical, and Christian sources on the theme of dominion." From: J. Cohen, 3).
[167] Num.32:22,29; Jos.18:1; 2 Sam.8:11; I Chr.22:18; II Chr.28:10; Neh.5:5; Esther 7:8; Jer.34:11,16; Mic.7:19; Zec.9:15.
[168] Lev. 25:43, 46, 53; Is. 14:6; Ezek. 34:4; I Kings 5:30, 9:23; II Chr. 8:10; I Kings 5:4; Ezek. 29:15, 34:4; Ps. 68:28, 72:8; Lev. 26:17; Is. 14:2; Ps. 110:2' Neh. 9:28; Judg. 5:13; Is. 41:2; Joel 4:13.
[169] Wendell Berry. *Standing by Words.* "Poetry and Place" (1983; Washington DC: Shoemaker and Hoard, 2005) 142-143. Myles Coverdale (1488-1568) worked off of Latin and German translations of the Bible, but... "If he was in fact (which has been questioned) the translator of the version of the Bible attributed to him, he is entitled to the credit for much of the noble language of the Authorized Version..." ("Coverdale," *The Oxford Companion to English Literature*, 1985 ed.). I'll also go into this a little more. If this (i.e. Coverdale, Pope, etc.) was once a camp in England or a remnant of more pan-European understanding of this verse then in any case it has become marginal for some time. The last concerted discussion of it in English speaking countries was probably the Distributist movement of G.K. Chesterton and Hilaire Belloc in the early twentieth century. Chesterton was

Catholic, as was Pope, and Catholic exegesis of this verse has probably been more conscious of the agricultural injunction than Protestant circles. Although the distinction is by no means absolute as Catholic discussion of it would probably be more in harkening back to the Medieval model, which bears similarities to the aristocratic or Homeric model, whereas Protestantism would probably be more akin to the decentralized model of Hesiod and the early Hebrews. Luther translated the verse of course, and I do not know if he wrote commentary on it. In general, Montmarquet says that Luther was socially conservative when it came to occupational subjects; he says that after the barbarian invasions that the early Medieval Church put the scale of virtue with agriculture first, then handi-craft, and then commerce, and that Luther stuck to the program in this area. (Montmarquet, 115). Obviously this changed in Protestant countries as time passed and later in Catholic countries as well, with an occupation in commerce and the professions becoming more socially desirable than earning a living off of agricultural land. Calvin's commentary on this verse is interesting. He has a conception of it something along the lines of Berry but his view is nuanced. See: John King. *Commentaries on the First Book of Moses by John Calvin.* Vol.1. (Grand Rapids, Mich.: Baker Book House, 1984) 97-100.

[170] Although in the second account man and woman are first in the Garden of Eden and the injunction comes after the Fall. To elaborate more on this pivotal verse one of the questions here is whether or not the source of food that God prescribes for humanity is cultivated plants or plants that grow in the wild. The verse that immediately follows the pivotal verse reads: "Then God said, 'I give you every seed-bearing plant on the face of the earth and every tree that has fruit with seed in it. And to all the beasts of the earth and all the birds of the air and all the creatures that move along the ground—everything that has the breath of life in it—I give every green plant for food.' And it was so." (Genesis 1.29) It is possible that this verse is in apposition to the pivotal verse and repeats what the injunction "to subdue" is referring to. If not then it is saying that wild plants are to be the food for men and women, although I argue that this is unlikely. Humans cannot forage like herbivores can and so if it is saying that humans are to live off of gathering wild plants then it certainly prescribes a menial existence. The first account of Creation in Genesis in which this verse lies does not mention the Garden of Eden as does the second and so this is not an idyllic situation where ample food is plucked from trees. Taken all together—especially in light of the rest of the Torah and the Old Testament—I agree that the verb "to subdue" means "to cultivate the earth" in this text.

[171] "St. Paul," *The Catholic Encyclopedia.* Vol.XI. (New York: Robert Appleton Co., 1911).

[172] This may be of less consequence environmentally than if any form of agrarianism developed in Western Christianity, but I think that it is still worth

discussion because it can raise some of the early factors that may have contributed to the eventual marginalization of the economic parts of the Bible in the West.
[173] The degree to which it took hold in the Byzantine Christianity would be an interesting subject.
[174] See Appendix B. Also of course I have to make the distinction here between the Catholic Church and Protestant Churches, but I am reluctant to get into it because I do not know the degree to which Catholicism and Protestantism have differed in this respect (the agrarian view of nature and economics). I recollect that the Catholic Church put up more of a fight when it came to accepting industrialism but see Montmarquet.
[175] "Historical Roots of Our Ecological Crisis", by Lynn White Jr. In: Cheryl Glotfelty and Harold Fromm. *The Ecocriticism Reader.: Landmarks of Literary Ecology*. (Athens and London, the University of Georgia Press, 1996).
[176] He asserts, "Especially in its Western form, Christianity is the most anthropocentric religion the world has seen.(p.9)" Also, "No new set of basic values has been accepted in our society to displace those of Christianity. Hence we shall continue to have a worsening ecologic crisis until we reject the Christian axiom that nature has no reason for existence save to serve man. (p.14)." Glotfely & Fromm, 9,14.
[177] And "We would seem to be headed toward conclusions unpalatable to many Christians. Since both *science* and *technology* are blessed words in our contemporary vocabulary, some may be happy at the notions, first, that, viewed historically, modern science is an extrapolation of natural theology, and second, that modern technology is at least partly to be explained as an Occidental, voluntarist realization of the Christian dogma of man's transcendence of, and rightful mastery over, nature." Glotfely and Fromm, 12. Or as he words it in another place, "The dynamism of religious devotion, shaped by the Judeo-Christian dogma of creation, gave it (science) impetus." Glotfelty and Fromm, 11-12.
[178] One of the main questions, if not the question, in environmentalism in my opinion is how to employ a large number of people in an ecological economy. History provides us with many examples of societies in which agriculture served this function, and in fact post-War societies are conspicuous for attempting otherwise. If we forget this it in turn takes the discussion into either the realm of mysticism where man is talked about as if he were still living in wild nature, or into the realm of essentially palliative measures in which the current industrial division of the natural and human communities is taken as a given. There is a plausible argument that a relatively sustainable balance between the industrial and agricultural sectors—which I call the industrial-agricultural economy—was achieved in countries like the United States and Canada before the Second World War. But the current technological-commercial economy on a global scale is

unprecedented therefore it is unknown whether or not such an economy can be ecological or not.

[179] Also Amos 3.4-12; Micah. 5.8; Nahum. 2.11-12.These are references where the writers speak intimately about the animals, arguing that they were familiar with their habits, whereas those listed in the text are direct references. .

[180] Glotfelty and Fromm, 12.

[181] "C.F. Whitley and Claus Westermann, among others, have held that because Gen. 1:28 reflects the terminology and ideology of ancient Near Eastern kingship, human rule must entail concern for the welfare of its subjects; kingship without responsibility was universally unacceptable." J. Cohen, 17.

[182] Furthermore, I broaden this to say that the tendency of certain modern technologies to replace other human functions i.e. telephones speaking face to face, televisions seeing in person—strikes me as Platonic. I want to clarify, however, that I am not advancing here that it has been the reading of Plato that has resulted directly in the development of modern science and technology. Rather what I am advocating is that it was familiarity with aspects of his philosophy, either directly or indirectly through other authors, that predisposed educated early modern Christians to accept science and its applications in technology.

[183] David Stockton. *The Gracchi*. (Oxford: Clarendon Press, 1979) 64.

[184] Stockton says, "The tribunates of Tiberius and his younger brother Gaius mark a watershed in the history of the later Roman republic." Stockton, 4. The fight surrounding this law reveal fundamental dynamics in Roman history.

[185] Thomas P. Govan. "Agrarian and Agrarianism: A Study in the Use and Abuse of Words" ,in *The Journal of Southern History,* (Vol. XXX, Feb.1964) 36.

[186] Govan., 36.

[187] Ibid., 36-39.

[188] Ibid., 39.

[189] Ibid., 40.

[190] Ibid., 39.

[191] For more regarding Berry's views on the Vanderbilt Agrarians, see: Wendell Berry. *A Continuous Harmony: Essays Cultural and Agricultural.* (1970 &1972; Washington D.C.: Shoemaker and Hoard, 2003) 64, 115.

[192] See Berry's *The Hidden Wound* (1989) for more on this subject.

[193] Wendell Berry, "The Agrarian Standard", *Orion,* Twentieth Anniversary Issue 2002.

[194] Montmarquet, viii.

[195] Od.1.190, 11.188, 17.18, 17.182, 22.47, ; Sophocles *Oedipus Tyrannus* 112, 1049; Ibid. *Electra* 313, 1051; Epicharmus 162; Euripies *Suppliant Women* 884; Thucydides 2.13 c.f 14; Plato *Laws* 881 C; Aristophanes *Frogs* 344; Xenophon *Memorabilia* 2.9; Ib. *Anabasis* 5.3,9.

[196] Aristophanes *Clouds* 43. There is also ἀγροτησ "a country-man, rustic": Eur. Or.1270; ἀγροτικόσ (adj.) "rustic": Eustathius Opuscula (ed. Tafel) (261.24).

[197] ἄγροικοσ: Plato *Phaedrus* 229 E cf. Isocrates 98 D; also Aristotle *Nichomahean Ethics* 7.3,9; ἀγροτερωσ (adv.): Plato, *Republic* 361 E; αγροτερον: Ibid, *Phaedrus* 260 D; ἀγροικία Ibid., *Gorgias* 461 C, *Republic* 560 D; also Aristotle *Nichomachen Ethics* 2.7, 13; ἀγροικίζομαι: Plato., *Theaetetus* 146 A; this verb also in Plutarch *Sulla* 6; Aristides I.491. All of these citations employ the negative sense.

[198] ἄγροικοσ: Aristophanes *Clouds* 628, 646; Ibid., *Acharnians* 674; ἀγρεῖος, Ibid., *Clouds* 655. *Clouds* is a play mocking Socrates as a corrupt teacher of rhetoric.

[199] And in fact Ischomachus is the one giving the respected philosophic figure advice.

[200] οἰκονομία "the management of a household or family, husbandry, thrift": Plat. Apol. 36B, Rep.498A, Xen. Oec.1.1; Arist. Eth. N.6.8,3, Pol.1.3-13; in plural: Plat. Rep.407B; Arist.G.A. 2.6,42. οἰκονομικόσ (adj.) "practiced in the management of a household or family": Plat. Alc.1.133E, Phaedr. 248D, Xen. Oec.1,3; Arist. Pol.1.1,2; hence "thrifty, frugal, economical": Xen. Mem. 4.4,39; Phylarch. 50. οἰκονομόσ "one who manages a household,= οἰκδεσπότησ, Xen. Oec. 1,2; Plat. Rep. 417A; also "a house-steward", being a slave: Corpus Inscriptionum (Böckhii) 2512; generally "a manager, administrator": Arist. Pol. 5.11,19; also could be a woman "a housekeeper, housewife": Phocyl. 3, Aesch. Ag. 155, Lysias. 92.22.

[201] Hdt. 4.109., 5.6; Dem.933.fin; in absol., Soph. O.T. 859; Eur, El. 75; Aristophanes Ach. 611.

[202] Hdt. 4.18; Ar. Pax 296; Plat. Phaedr.276B.

Χενοπηον υσεσ τηε τσο τερμσ τουετηερ αὐτ. γεωργοί (Xen. Oec. 5, 4).

[204] For a more thorough airing please see Montmarquet.

[205] Montmarquet, 7.

[206] The increased attention that scholars have given to Berry indicates that this is the case. Kimberly K. Smith's *Wendell Berry and the Agrarian Tradition* is an example of this, as well as other studies (see in Bibliography I: Logsdon (2007), Ochiai (2004), Summerhill (2005), Freyfogle (2001, 2003, 2006, 2007), Wirzba (2004) etc....). Smith highlights the most important legacy that Wendell Berry's writing will leave. She writes, "By importing an environmental sensibility into traditional agrarianism, Berry and his followers have revived and transformed a major branch of the American intellectual heritage." Kimberly K. Smith. *Wendell Berry and the Agrarian Tradition* (Kansas: University of Kansas Press, 2003) 2.

VDM publishing house ltd.

Scientific Publishing House

offers

free of charge publication

of current academic research papers, Bachelor´s Theses, Master's Theses, Dissertations or Scientific Monographs

If you have written a thesis which satisfies high content as well as formal demands, and you are interested in a remunerated publication of your work, please send an e-mail with some initial information about yourself and your work to info@vdm-publishing-house.com.

Our editorial office will get in touch with you shortly.

VDM Publishing House Ltd.
Meldrum Court 17.
Beau Bassin
Mauritius
www.vdm-publishing-house.com